FLYING SCOTSMAN

THE EXTRAORDINARY STORY OF THE WORLD'S MOST FAMOUS TRAIN

Above No. 4472 *Flying Scotsman*, still in 1924 condition, passes Potters Bar with the 1.55pm up Leeds and Harrogate express in January 1926.

FLYING SCOTSMAN

THE EXTRAORDINARY STORY OF THE WORLD'S MOST FAMOUS TRAIN

Aurum
Press

ANDREW RODEN

Quarto is the authority on a wide range of topics.

Quarto educates, entertains and enriches the lives of our readers—enthusiasts and lovers of hands-on living.

www.QuartoKnows.com

First published in Great Britain

2007 by Aurum Press Ltd

74—77 White Lion Street

London N1 9PF

www.aurumpress.co.uk

This edition first published in 2016 by Aurum Press Ltd.

Copyright © Andrew Roden 2007, 2015, 2016

Design © Aurum Press 2016

A catalogue record for this book is available from the British Library.

ISBN 978 1 78131 613 9

2016 2018 2020 2019 2017

FLYING SCOTSMAN

LEAVES KING'S CROSS (LONDON) 10.0.a.m. EVERY WEEK-DAY

CONTENTS

Opposite The London and North Eastern Railway named *Flying Scotsman* after its 1920s flagship train of the same name. Both were promoted with brilliant creativity.

Above Luggage labels also promoted 'The Flying Scotsman'. The upper one shows the famous locomotive while the lower depicts one of the streamlined 'A4s' which superseded *Flying Scotsman* on the most prestigious expresses.

PREFACE

In the early 1950s, *Flying Scotsman*, the world's most famous steam locomotive, was sent from her old stamping grounds on the line north from King's Cross to help haul passenger trains from Leicester to London Marylebone on the old Great Central Main Line.

One day, she was rostered to take over the Sheffield to Marylebone 'South Yorkshire Pullman' from Leicester to the capital. It was a fairly routine duty, and although an extra couple of coaches had been added as it was a public holiday, it was well within the capabilities of this Brunswick-green racehorse.

Problems had been reported with *Flying Scotsman's* injectors the day before, but by the time the young fireman, Ken Issitt, joined the locomotive at the Leicester shed they had been resolved.

The Gresley-designed locomotive rapidly gathered pace on her way south from Leicester, getting to grips with her load, and cantering down the flat and level Great Central Main Line. Soon after it passed Charwelton in Northamptonshire, however, the right-hand injector began to leak water, a sure sign that something was awry. *Flying Scotsman* would normally have been able to keep pace with the steaming rate on just one injector, but Issitt kept having to supplement it with short bursts from the left-hand injector. Things got worse, and the right-hand injector failed completely just after the train went past Aylesbury. Although this wasn't dangerous, it meant that Issitt and Cyril Chamberlain, the driver, would have to work hard to conserve steam in order to avoid draining the boiler.

The situation worsened further. The left-hand – and hitherto reliable – injector started playing up. Issitt tried everything he could think of to get it working, but as the train passed Wendover, near Aylesbury, that too failed. With no way of getting water into the boiler, things were looking serious. By now, Issitt had stopped firing, but the burning coals in the firebox would boil all the water away, and that could lead to only one thing: a catastrophic boiler explosion. Drastic action was called for.

'The fire had to come out pretty damn quick,' recalls Issitt. 'Bear in mind that there's something like 41 square feet of grate area in the firebox and at least two tons of burning coal in there, and you can see the problem we had.

'I began winding the grate down while Cyril struggled with the injector. He set the engine coasting with the regulator barely open.'

Issitt took the long fire shovel from the tender and started pushing the fire from the firebox into the ashpan. As *Flying Scotsman* continued running, burning coals showered from her underside as if she was bleeding. The vegetation on the embankments and cuttings – despite being well tended – was soon ablaze.

The two men were doing everything within their power, and Issitt pushed himself to the limits of exhaustion frantically trying to remove the heat source from the boiler in order to save their locomotive and the passengers on the train.

'The fire shovel was beginning to become soft and bend with the heat. The water level had disappeared in the glass. We looked anxiously into the firebox to see if the lead plugs in its roof had melted, and for the telltale hiss of steam telling us how near we were to disaster and the need for us to run for our lives. We were seconds away from oblivion.'

Unless Chamberlain could get the injectors working and get water into the boiler, the lead plugs in the firebox roof would, as Issitt points out, melt, venting steam into the firebox to warn the crew of danger and relieve the increasingly explosive pressure. However, this would be no solution – merely a way of buying the crew a few precious extra seconds. After the lead plugs had melted, the water would fall below the copper surface of the inner firebox, which ordinarily was kept from melting only by the water that surrounded it absorbing the heat. If the firebox had started to melt, the boiler would have been completely out of control. Anything could happened – it could have imploded, sending the white-hot steam back into the cab and the train; it could have exploded, sending the boiler flying off *Flying Scotsman's* chassis; or any one of a number of other catastrophes could have wrecked the engine. The only certainty is that Issitt and Chamberlain – and many of their passengers – would have been killed or seriously injured.

With the train now coasting at 40mph, Chamberlain continued to hammer, kick, coax and curse the injectors. There seemed nothing wrong with them. He and Issitt needed a miracle.

They got one: suddenly the injectors started to pick up water and send it into the boiler. There was no rhyme or reason for it, but Chamberlain wasn't going to worry about that for the moment. He shouted across to his mate: 'I've got it working!'

'Thank God,' said a relieved Issitt.

Flying Scotsman was nursed to London, arriving just five minutes late. She was clearly not in a fit state to return to Leicester until the problem had been sorted once and for all. Issitt was sufficiently intrigued by the day's difficulties to find out what had caused them. 'There was nothing wrong with the injectors. They separated the engine from the tender for inspection and found algae and rust had blocked the strainers in the tender.

'When the fitters drained the tender, they found three buckets of live fish – roach, bream, rudd – all swimming around happily, living off the algae in the tender!'

It may sound like a fishy tale, but the Leicester shed took its water from a canal through a nine-inch pipe. The fish had been sucked up through this and sent straight into *Flying Scotsman's* tender, where they happily feasted on the algae. They could never have known just how close they came to destroying a national icon.

On another day, Issitt and Chamberlain would rightly have been acclaimed as heroes, but for them, all that lay ahead now was a trip back to Leicester behind a lesser engine. If ever a steam locomotive was to prove the cat with nine lives of the railways, it was *Flying Scotsman*. She had just used up her first. The following fifty years would see her need all the others.

Previous pages This oil painting by Mike Jeffries shows a typical scene of the 1920s with No. 4472 *Flying Scotsman* hauling her namesake train. Designed by Nigel Gresley in 1922 and built in Doncaster Works in 1923 she was the first steam locomotive to verifiably reach 100mph.

Below In the 1950s *Flying Scotsman* was cascaded to the Great Central Main Line along with other 'A3s'. On 5 July 1952 she heads towards London Marylebone on 'The South Yorkshireman' near Lutterworth.

STARTING LINES

January 1963 was cold. Temperatures fell to -16C, the River Thames froze over, and even the sea froze in Herne Bay. Cliff Richard was doing his best to cheer up shivering Britain with 'Bachelor Boy' at number one, but it wasn't a promising start to a momentous year that would eventually see the Beatles release their first album and President Kennedy assassinated.

On 14 January 1963, in a filthy, soot-encrusted shed just a few hundred yards away, near York Way, a man stood back from his charge. It had taken huge effort, but after hours of patient and determined work, she was ready.

Her big, black nose shone in the weak, early morning sunlight, and her steel limbs glistened with a sheen of lubricating oil and paraffin just a few molecules thick. From perhaps 6 feet above the man's head came the sound of steel on steel, followed by the grating of cold, polished shovel against frozen, unwilling coal. A quick shuffle of feet, then a clang as the bottom of the shovel's blade bounced off an iron casting protecting vital copper, propelling its contents 11 feet forward to land on a precisely selected patch of gently burning coal.

The man walked to his right, savouring, for the last time, the huge sweep of giant wheels that had propelled this beast at 110mph and made her the fastest in the world for a while: wheels that had been the first to run the 393 miles non-stop from London to Edinburgh, claiming another record in the process. Looming over the wheels, like a thoroughbred's body over its legs, was a giant Brunswick green-painted boiler. In its day this had been among the most advanced in the world, and even now, there was little to match it for sustained, high-power output. Halfway along the beast's length, gently describing an arc over the middle set of big wheels, was the cast-brass nameplate, the letters

equally spaced along its length – the most recognised name anywhere in the world: *Flying Scotsman*.

Flying Scotsman was no stranger to the history books, thanks to her glory days at the Wembley Exhibition in 1924, and two spectacular record-breaking runs in the 1920s and 1930s. She was as close as the railway could get to a national icon: a name recognised by millions, a name whose romance and speed summed up the age of steam. That age was almost over.

But not quite. Today was to be *Flying Scotsman's* last in front-line service. Her career of forty years had come to a close, not because she was incapable of the work required of her – far from it: recent developments initiated at her King's Cross home, known as 'Top Shed', had made her one of the most efficient steam locomotives in the world. Instead, a faceless bureaucrat had decreed that she and her kin stood in the way of progress and must be replaced by the latest products from the blast furnace of technology. Never mind that the diesel locomotives that would replace her were unreliable, expensive and little more powerful: this was Progress, and that was all there was to it.

Standing next to the locomotive, shivering in the cold, was a former dive-bomber pilot in his early forties. Tall and well built, with perhaps a little middle-aged spread, he had

a neatly trimmed moustache, and, though his hair was thinning, he nonetheless carried himself with the assurance and poise derived from extreme wealth. He was a member of the British Railways area board responsible for King's Cross, and he had risked his career to save this iconic locomotive from the scrap man's torch. He'd paid a princely sum for the privilege, and he still wasn't quite sure what he was going to do with this giant steam locomotive – but what he did know was that the nation would mourn her passing if nobody had stepped in to save her. By the end of *Flying Scotsman's* journey to Doncaster that day (where she would be taken off the train and replaced by one of her slightly less glamorous sisters for the final leg to Leeds), Alan Pegler would own this locomotive: the first private citizen in Britain ever to possess a front-line express steam locomotive in his own right.

Not surprisingly, Pegler was a popular character with the newsreel and television crews shivering with him at Top Shed. He was a swashbuckling, buccaneering character with a posh accent and slightly raffish demeanour. Why, they asked, had he bought his own steam locomotive? The insinuation that this was merely the whim of a man with money to burn was clear. Pegler was equally clear: he'd not saved *Flying Scotsman* for himself: he'd saved her for the nation, as the nation was unwilling to do so itself. He couldn't, he said, let this wonderful machine be scrapped.

Time ticked towards the Leeds-bound train's departure time of 13:15, and like mourners at a wake, people from all over London and beyond came to pay their respects. It started as a trickle, then became a stream and then a torrent. Every vantage point at King's Cross was packed with people who ordinarily couldn't care less about railways, all wanting to see this momentous occasion: *Flying Scotsman's* last departure from the station that she had been running to for almost all her career.

Flying Scotsman pulled away from Top Shed with Pegler on the footplate. Once on the main line, she reversed back into King's Cross station to be coupled to her train. As first the screw coupling linked locomotive with train, then the

left *Flying Scotsman* stands on Doncaster shed just after her overhaul for new owner Alan Pegler on 19 May 1963.

Above Once Alan Pegler had acquired *Flying Scotsman* he ran her
on rail tours all over Britain. This scene at London King's Cross in
October 1963 was typical of the reception the locomotive garnered
– even though steam locomotives were still in main line service.

vital train brake pipe and finally the equally vital steam heat pipes were attached, anticipation reached a climax. Pegler stood on the front buffer beam to acknowledge the crowds who had come to see the locomotive that would soon be his. He stood with restrained dignity, doubtless glad of the warming heat of *Flying Scotsman's* smokebox on his back. Before long, the guard was ready to whistle the train's departure to Leeds and Pegler hurried to the footplate. At the shrill of the guard's whistle, the driver opened the cylinder drain cocks, then the regulator slightly, before releasing the brakes. After a moment the high-pressure steam reached *Flying Scotsman's* gigantic cylinders, and she inched forward, her great wheels sweeping round faster and faster as she got to grips with her heavy load.

The crowds waved their hats and cheered as the train pulled away from the platform and watched as she entered Gasworks Tunnel for the last time on her way north. They waited until the train's tail light had disappeared in the gloom and the distinctive sound of this three-cylinder locomotive had faded into the hustle and bustle of the city. This really did feel like the end of a golden age for those lucky enough to witness it.

Ever since then, *Flying Scotsman* has proved an enduring icon of the steam railway, the most popular locomotive in the world, the one which, if you ask somebody with no interest in railways to name a steam engine, they will name. She's become such a recognised name that it's now almost impossible to have a rational discussion about railway

history, and particularly steam locomotive history, without her looming large – and this is something I've always questioned. I'm not old enough to have seen the glory days of the 1920s and 1930s, the brief renaissance of the 1950s, or the sad decline of the 1960s – but even the most cursory look around the wonderful National Railway Museum in York proves that there were faster, more powerful, and more modern steam locomotives than *Flying Scotsman*. Why has she become known as the greatest steam locomotive of all when others, such as her speed record-holding cousin *Mallard*, surely deserve many more plaudits?

Perhaps it's that *Flying Scotsman* so effortlessly embraces the old and the modern: nobody would ever mistake her for anything other than a steam locomotive, yet in her cleanliness of line and unfussy design, she looks modern almost a century after she was built. Perhaps her greatest achievement is that she paved the way for other designs to set new standards in power, speed and reliability. She arrived too late to dominate the great 'Races to the North', and too soon for the locomotive arms races of the 1930s; without her, though, advances such as non-stop, long-distance trains and high-speed, lightweight flyers might not have happened. The tale of how *Flying Scotsman* came to be, and how she has become so universally recognised and adored is one of human ingenuity and brilliance, of scheming politics, and of how, just occasionally, the seemingly impossible can happen. If her designer, Nigel Gresley could see her now, he'd be delighted.

2

GENESIS

In 1919 Doncaster was a typical northern industrial town. Huge chimneys dotted the skyline, belching out thick, soot-laden smoke; hooters summoned workers to their factories, and everywhere was the smell of burning coal. It was a scene that had changed little for fifty years, and at the centre of the town was the locomotive, carriage and wagon works of the Great Northern Railway (GNR).

It was manufacturing on a gigantic scale. Steam hammers whistled upwards, paused for a second, and thundered down on to white-hot billets of steel in a crash and a shower of sparks. Expert craftsmen toiled over metal and wood, turning raw, unwilling materials into the precision-made components that, once assembled into their final form, delivered goods and carried passengers over a region ranging from London through Hertfordshire and into the flat countryside of Cambridgeshire, Nottinghamshire, Lincolnshire and Yorkshire. The noise had to be heard to be believed, and above all this din rang the riveting of the boilermakers, their work vital in assembling the boilers of the GNR's steam locomotives. It was organised chaos, and, after years of wartime armaments production,

Opposite above Doncaster Works was the engineering hub of the Great Northern Railway (GNR) – and despite extensive use of machinery, depended on highly skilled manual labour.

Opposite below Coach repairing at Doncaster works, South Yorkshire, c. 1916. The GNR – which owned the works at the time – built its carriages largely from wood. The beautifully varnished teak finish would become a signature of its successor, London and North Eastern Railway (LNER). Doncaster Works opened in 1853 and at the time this picture was taken employed at least 3,500 workers.

Right Sir Nigel Gresley, Chief Mechanical Engineer of the LNER, c. 1930s. Born in Edinburgh in 1876, Gresley was first apprenticed to the London and North Western Railway at Crewe, before working for the Lancashire and Yorkshire Railway at Horwich Works, where he rose to the post of Assistant Superintendent in 1904. He then joined the GNR, and by 1911 was Chief Mechanical Engineer, responsible for the design of locomotives and carriages. He continued in this post when the GNR was absorbed into the LNER in 1923, and was knighted for his services to the railway industry in 1936.

Doncaster Works was turning its hand to its primary occupation.

It wasn't all noise, though. As with every big industrial site, there were odd oases of quiet, and in one of these, Nigel Gresley, the Chief Mechanical Engineer (CME) of the railway, was deep in thought. A vicar's son of Norman ancestry and from a privileged background, he was a giant of a man, comfortably over 6 feet tall, and strongly built. He was keen on sports, and by all accounts had boundless enthusiasm. His friends, ironically, called him 'Tiny'. Pictures of him are few, but show a man with thick, wavy hair and a moustache. His face was soft but not round, and he looked more than anything like a kindly uncle. Although, at forty-three, he was the youngest CME of a major railway in Britain, he had toiled long and hard to reach his position: for the moment, he was stumped by one challenge in particular.

In the eighteen months or so he had been in the job before the First World War, it had become apparent that the most powerful passenger locomotives in the GNR fleet, the 'Atlantics' designed by his predecessor Henry Ivatt, would soon be hard pressed to haul heavier and faster trains. During the war, loads had got heavier still, but, because speeds were restricted, the 'Atlantics' were able to perform adequately. Now, with a return to pre-war schedules imminent, and with a new generation of passenger coaches on the horizon, the express passenger locomotives would need to be replaced sooner rather than later with something much faster and more

powerful. The question was: 'with what?' There were no easy answers.

Gresley at least had the benefit of other people's experience to guide him, and by the end of the First World War, pretty much every problem that the steam railway could face had been met – and conquered – somewhere in the world. In Britain at the time most passenger locomotives had eight or ten wheels, plus a tender carrying coal and water, which they hauled immediately behind the cab. At the front they typically had four wheels in a sub-frame called a bogie to guide them round curves, then four or six wheels coupled together and linked to gigantic pistons, and in some cases, a pair of small wheels underneath the cab to offer some support. In the 'Whyte notation' system, this meant that the locomotives were described as 4-4-2 – or 'Atlantics'. Gresley wanted to go one step further, to a 4-6-2, or 'Pacific', which offered the possibility of a quantum leap in boiler size and power, but in Britain at least, nobody had yet built a successful 'Pacific'.

Gresley's love of engineering and passion for railways meant that he was always destined for a role on the iron road. Moreover, his varied experience had given him the knowledge to filter out the best practice from other railways and apply it to the GNR. He started his career as an apprentice with the London and North Western Railway – the biggest player in the West Coast alliance – at Crewe Works, one of the finest locomotive works in the world. This was in 1893, a time when the famous 'Races to the North' between companies operating the East Coast route from King's Cross and their West Coast competitors working out of Euston, had provided a spur for improved designs. Gresley made the most of this, and then by the turn of the century, he moved north to the Lancashire and Yorkshire Railway, which was building some extremely advanced locomotives for the time. He worked first in the drawing office at Horwich and then the test room and materials workshop. After that he moved to Blackpool, where he became running shed foreman and gained a practical understanding of day-to-day railway operation. He moved on to take over the carriage and wagon department at the GNR's Doncaster works in 1905. This effectively made him the company's engineering number two – and his senior, Henry Ivatt, was due to retire by 1911.

Ivatt had transformed the GNR from a traditional Victorian railway into a mid-table, premier-league player with some modern and extremely capable designs. Many express locomotives (except on the Great Western

Below Two of Gresley's predecessors, Henry Alfred Ivatt and Archibald Sturrock stand by a 'K1' 0-8-0 in 1903. Gresley was tasked with modernising and upgrading the GNR's fleet to cope with rising passenger and goods traffic.

Opposite This typical nineteenth-century scene on the East Coast Main Line near Hadley Wood shows how much the railway scene changed in a generation. The Stirling-designed 'single' wheelers struggled for traction and even their successors had difficulties.

"THE FLYING SCOTCHMAN", GREAT NORTHERN RLY.

The Knight Series, No. 599.

Railway, GWR) were 4-4-0s, but Ivatt added a pair of trailing wheels to make them 4-4-2s, which meant that the engine could be longer and the firebox area bigger, allowing the engines to create more steam. In the early years of the twentieth century, these 'Atlantics' were competent if hungry performers, able to keep schedules with the loads then common. But one of the reasons that by 1919 the GNR needed more powerful engines was that Gresley had designed and built a new generation of carriages that transformed the passenger experience, being much more airy than most in use on the GNR, smoother riding and running more freely.

In 1911 Gresley was just thirty-five years old, and his skill and good work as Ivatt's number two ensured his succession: the youngest CME among his contemporaries by a considerable margin. For the new CME of a railway company, the temptation is always to produce the fastest, most glamorous engines possible – the express passenger locomotives. In today's road-dominated society, though, it is very difficult to appreciate how totally dominant the railways were for transporting goods a century ago. For the GNR, that meant it had to move coal from Yorkshire, fish from Grimsby, bricks from Peterborough, produce from Lincolnshire, and everything and anything else that anyone in its territory wanted moving. These were the trains which really made money.

Gresley's first locomotives therefore had to be goods engines, and he simply built further batches of Ivatt's designs: why reinvent the wheel for the sake of it? The first of Gresley's own designs were of the 2-6-0, or 'Mogul' type designed to perform on a range of duties from goods to passenger trains. Gresley had planned to build a new generation of express locomotives in 1915, but the First World War forced non-essential construction to be postponed, and Doncaster Works was turned over to the war effort. (Gresley himself was a member of the engineering committee of the Ministry of Food – and was awarded a CBE for his efforts in 1920.)

Initial plans were for something with a bigger boiler than Ivatt's 'Atlantics', and an extra pair of driving wheels. The 4-6-2 arrangement gave 50 per cent more grip and allowed a much bigger boiler and firebox to be carried.

The problem was that building cylinders outside the wheels able to cope with that much steam presented a problem: they would obliterate platform edges from King's Cross to York. The solution was to use the space between the frames to hold more cylinders. There was nothing new in this; most locomotives on the GNR had their two cylinders between the frames, and other railways were starting to use four cylinders to cope with the output offered by bigger boilers.

This seemed the way forward, so Gresley used the lull in building caused by the war to fit a 'Large Atlantic' with four cylinders to see the effect. It worked mechanically but Gresley wasn't convinced about the need for four cylinders. But if four cylinders weren't the answer, what was? There

Below The first 'Pacific' built by the GNR was No. 1470 *Great Northern*. This picture was taken either in 1922 or very shortly after the 1923 Grouping that created the LNER.

was no way that the board of directors would countenance making clearances big enough for the huge outside cylinders needed for a larger boiler with just two of them, which left only one option: to go for three. At the time the use of three cylinders was not unknown in Britain, but it was far from the norm. Theoretically it offered the ability to use all the steam a big boiler could generate and would offer extremely smooth delivery of power.

Gresley began by experimenting with a three-cylinder version of his heavy freight locomotives, which proved highly successful. A first was the use of 'conjugated valve gear': an arrangement almost unique to Gresley by which the actions of the valves in the two cylinders outside the wheels move the valves on the middle cylinder between the wheels. This makes maintenance easier under good

conditions and gives more space between the wheels to deal with the piston from the cylinder. But, if Gresley's vision of a new generation of express locomotives was going to work, the valve gear would have to work at high speeds. And this needed to be proved quickly, because by 1919 Ivatt's 'Large Atlantics' were really struggling with the loadings post-war conditions demanded of them. Before he was prepared to build his big new design, though, he wanted to confirm that his plans for new larger boilers would work in practice.

Gresley's ambitions for big three-cylinder locomotives depended on teaming a free-steaming boiler with a chassis similar to that of his latest freight locomotives. So he built another type of 'Mogul' which combined the two. The 'K', with the widest boiler then fitted to a British locomotive,

"FLYING SCOTSMAN," L.N.E.R., 4472.   4-6-2.   3-CYLINDER ENGINE.   TYPE A.1.

ONE OF THE WORLD'S MOST POPULAR ENGINES, AND USED FOR THE FAMOUS LONDON TO ABERDEEN RUN.

GAUGE OF TRACK	4 FT. 8½ INS.	FIRE BOX WIDTH	7 FT. 9 INS.
CYLINDERS	20 INS. x 26 INS.	TUBES	Number 168. Diameter 2¼ INS.
DRIVING WHEEL DIAMETER	6 FT. 8 INS.		32 5¼ INS.
BOILER INSIDE DIAMETER	6 FT. 3 5/8 INS.	8-WHEELED CORRIDOR TENDER.	
PRESSURE	180 LBS.	CAPACITY WATER	5000 GALLONS
FIRE BOX LENGTH	9 FT. 5¼ INS.	COAL	9 TONS

HOW LOCOMOTIVES ARE CONFIGURED

In 1900, American engineer Frederick Whyte devised a system to describe the different wheel arrangements of steam locomotives, and it is still used in Britain today. The first number refers to the leading wheels of a locomotive, the second to the number of driving wheels and the third to the trailing wheels. *Flying Scotsman* is a 4-6-2, and under Whyte's system this means it has four wheels in a bogie supporting the front of the locomotive, six driving wheels and a pair at the rear supporting the cab and firebox. The tender carrying the water and coal is not included. For tank locomotives that carry their coal and water without a tender, the suffix T is used at the end, with variations for saddle tanks (ST) and pannier tanks (PT). The system isn't perfect: some locomotives were of the 2-2-2-2 type, which could imply two leading wheels, two sets of driving wheels and a pair of trailing wheels or two sets of leading wheels carried independently of a bogie, a pair of driving wheels, and two trailing wheels. To remove these ambiguities with diesel and electric locomotives Britain adopted the UIC system with numbers and letters is used which identifies which axles (rather than wheels) are powered and whether they are coupled together.

proved successful, but could the principles it embodied be used on an express locomotive? By 1922, Gresley was ready to put his ideas to the test. At that time, British experience with 'Pacifics' was limited to one unsuccessful prototype built by the GWR. Could he, and the GNR, really afford to take such a gigantic risk? Gresley looked overseas to see the latest American developments.

Back in 1911 the American Locomotive Company (ALCO) had built a prototype express locomotive for possible sale to railways across the United States and Canada, and very quickly the Pennsylvania Railroad based its 'K4' design on it. The 'K4' was a 'Pacific' designed for very high power at high speeds. It was designed to cruise at 60mph, and in the event, proved comfortable cruising at 80mph. The 'K4', like most American designs, was *way* too big to fit under bridges and alongside platforms in Britain. But that didn't matter: the proportions were right, and those *could* be adapted to fit the British loading gauge. This is what Gresley decided to do for his new express locomotives.

All the elements Gresley had spent the past few years working towards were now in place, and Doncaster Works was ready, willing and able to deliver something spectacular. After all, it would be the GNR's swansong, and they wanted to ensure that the venerable old lady went out in a blaze of glory.

Opposite *Flying Scotsman* postcard, No. 1274.

Above Nigel Gresley based his 'A1' design on the Pennsylvania Railroad's 'K4' 4-6-2. These locomotives were powerful and fast – and although they were far to big to run in Britain, Gresley's design had very similar proportions.

It was a swan-song for the GNR, and just about every other railway company in Britain, because of an impending restructuring of the industry. The railways were utterly exhausted after the First World War. They had performed prodigiously, moving everything needed to sustain a four-year struggle, and maintenance of locomotives, coaches, wagons and track had suffered. They needed time and money to catch up, but they were given neither. The government, impressed with the way the railways had operated under state control during the war, wanted to rationalise the huge number of railway companies, preferably into one. It had a clear choice – nationalise, or leave market forces to exert their will. So, after lengthy deliberations, which initially envisaged a hybrid of seven regional companies in 1919, it was finally decided to merge almost all of Britain's railways into four (now known as the

Grouping) from 1923, with a proviso that nationalisation could take place twenty-five years later.

All of this was in the imminent future when, in April 1922, Doncaster Works released a giant of an express engine, the first fruit of Gresley's experiments. She bore the number 1470 and above her giant driving wheels wore the proud name *Great Northern*. By British standards she was enormous, and clearly based on the proportions of the 'K4'. After initial tests she went into service between Doncaster and London and performed with flying colours. The new class of locomotive was known as 'A1', and never has such a suitable name been given to a design. Gresley was about to enter locomotive designer superstardom.

Later that year, *Great Northern* acquired a sister, No. 1471 *Sir Frederick Banbury*, named after a director of the GNR implacably opposed to the Grouping that was to

come. In the run-up to the Grouping, in September 1922, she hauled a special train between London and Grantham weighing 100 tons more than the heaviest allowed on the GNR – to the fastest time allowed for 'The Flying Scotsman' train (known officially then as 'The Special Scotch Express'). It was a powerful statement of intent and capability, and the purse strings of the GNR's board of directors were loosened for the final time: they ordered a production batch of ten 'A1s'. The first wouldn't be delivered until after the Grouping, and she wouldn't even be named – but even before the first metal was cut, she was given the number 1472. The world didn't know it, but in the heart of Yorkshire, the finest artistry Doncaster has ever produced was taking shape in the GNR's works: an icon that within just five years would become a legend.

Below Old and new on the East Coast Main Line: this painting by F. Moore shows the second 'A1', No. 1471 *Sir Frederick Banbury*, next to Stirling 'Single' No. 1 of 1870. The difference in size between the generations of motive power is stark, as is the less fussy and more industrial design. F. Moore was the collective name of a studio of artists operating in the first two decades of the twentieth century. They produced many paintings and painted photographs of steam locomotives prior to the advent of colour photography.

3

THE GREAT SHOW

In January 1923 the planned Grouping of Britain's railway companies into four regional giants finally happened. This was the year Howard Carter discovered the tomb of Tutankhamun, the year the BBC received its licence to broadcast, and for those rich enough to afford a radio, the year when they could buy a copy of the *Radio Times* for the princely sum of tuppence. It was a long, long time ago.

The airlines were making their first faltering lurches into the skies, carrying rich and daring passengers in what were converted First World War bombers that struggled to reach 100mph. For most, however, the prospect of flying – or indeed driving a car – was unthinkably distant: the overwhelming majority of Britons were far too poor to even dream of such things.

With all this happening, it's small wonder that when the first production 'A1', No. 1472, emerged from Doncaster Works on 24 February, the world didn't sit up and take notice. Nonetheless the day marked the completion of the first of Gresley's flagship design in series production – the first new express locomotive of the newly formed London and North Eastern Railway (LNER). No. 1472 cost £7,944: a trifle today, but a serious investment at a time when £1,000 a year was a massive wage that only some could dream of. As the first of the new 'Pacifics' to be delivered after the Grouping, she was presented to the LNER's directors in a private ceremony at Marylebone station.

The LNER, into which the Great Northern Railway (GNR) was now subsumed, was a colossus whose arms stretched from London throughout East Anglia, up to Newcastle and Edinburgh, the very farthest tip of Scotland, and even across the Pennines to Manchester: it was, by any measure, a massive undertaking, exceeded in size only marginally by its West Coast Main Line rival, the London, Midland and Scottish Railway (LMS).

Below *Flying Scotsman* stands new at Doncaster shed in 1923 shortly after construction. She was renumbered 4472 the following year.

Opposite below On 21 April 1925 *Flying Scotsman* is moved sideways from her track into position for exhibition at Wembley.

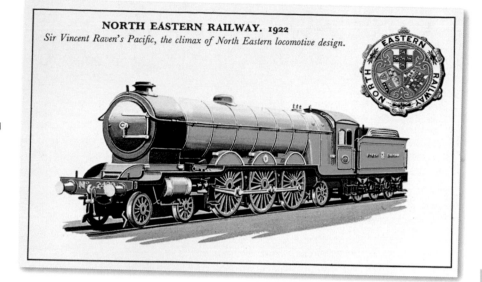

NORTH EASTERN RAILWAY. 1922

Sir Vincent Raven's Pacific, the climax of North Eastern locomotive design.

One of this giant's biggest headaches was to decide who should be its Chief Mechanical Engineer (CME). This person would have the enviable task of controlling engineering matters from Stratford in London to the Moray Firth, and the destinies of 7,400 locomotives. This appointment was not a simple matter, because Gresley faced two other extremely capable candidates. The most senior was John Robinson, the CME of the Great Central, who had provided it with a wide range of really good locomotives, and had proved far from afraid to innovate. His heavy freight design,

in particular, was as close as the railways got at that time to a national standard. The other candidate was Sir Vincent Raven of the North Eastern Railway. Raven had also proved he could walk the walk as well as talking the talk and, at almost the same time as the GNR introduced the 'A1s', had launched his own design of 'Pacific', No. 2400.

Despite the seniority of Robinson and Raven, the former probably tilted the tables in Gresley's favour by withdrawing from the contest on the grounds of age, and recommending the GNR's young CME as the best choice.

Even so, it can't have been an easy call for the LNER directors. They picked Gresley, gambling on his potential rather than on what he had delivered to date – but they unquestionably got the decision absolutely right. Raven was said to have been so disgusted by the decision that he emigrated. His son-in-law, Edward Thompson, was disappointed that Gresley got the job and was ultimately to wreak what many consider to be revenge in the 1940s.

While there was much reorganisation to do, one of the most crucial tasks for the engineering teams was to decide which of the two new express locomotive designs should be continued – Gresley's 'A1', or Raven's equivalent. In June 1923 a series of comparative trials between Gresley's 1472 and Raven's 2400 took place. By and large, performance was adequate for both – but, crucially, Gresley's design offered a 10 per cent saving in coal consumption, and was far better designed from a maintenance point of view, thanks to the conjugated valve gear.

Clearly, Gresley might naturally favour his own designs, but this shows his open-mindedness in being willing to evaluate his options. In truth, it was always likely that Gresley's design would win. It was based on rational development, whereas Raven, possibly out of a sense of rivalry with his younger counterpart, simply expanded one of his existing designs, when a fresh approach might have worked better. Still, there's no denying that Raven's 'Pacifics' were elegant machines that were able to fulfil their duties for the next decade or so.

The Empire Exhibition of 1924 was a classically British response to the problem that, having won the greatest of all wars up to that time, the country was now suffering a crisis of confidence. The British Empire, one must remember, was very much the *British Empire* at the time, and demanded respect. So a vast exhibition showing off the glories of the biggest empire the world had ever seen was planned for West London at Wembley. The British were going to have fun, and they were jolly well going to have it in style. And of course, as the country which invented the railways, perhaps the greatest contribution of the English-speaking world to date, it would be remiss not to showcase the latest developments.

Below As preparations for the British Empire Exhibition at Wembley gathered pace, No. 1472 is shunted into the site by Great Central Railway 'L1' 2-6-4T No. 342, early in 1924. *Flying Scotsman* was chosen because she had failed in service and needed repairs.

To that end, the organisers scoured the railways of Britain for the latest developments. Above all, two stood out. The first was Gresley's new 'Pacific' locomotive, the biggest passenger locomotive in Britain, and one of the most elegant pieces of engineering sculpture there has ever been. The second was the latest locomotive from the Great Western Railway (GWR), the smaller, but equally perfectly formed *Caerphilly Castle*. They were, and are, gorgeous.

The GWR had the name for its exhibit decided, but for the nascent LNER, the question was which locomotive to send, and what to do with it. In 1923 the company had finally made official what for something like fifty years had been unofficial: the 10:00 departure from King's Cross to Edinburgh was named 'The Flying Scotsman'. The question

Below The British Empire Exhibition was opened by King George V on St George's Day, 23 April 1924. This image shows the Indian Pavilion from the Boating Lake.

Following pages This plan of the Empire Exhibition shows how vast the site was and how visitors could get to and around it.

THE WEMBLEY EXHIBITION OF 1924/25

Although *Flying Scotsman* was one of the star exhibits at the Empire Exhibition in 1924 and 1925 the show wasn't designed just for railway exhibits. An exhibition showcasing the strength and breadth of the British Empire had been under consideration since before the Great War but it came together in the early 1920s. A vast site was chosen at Wembley, Middlesex, and the aim was to stimulate trade and strengthen bonds between Britain and her colonies and dominions. It was opened by King George VI on April 23 1924, cost £12 million and was claimed to be the largest exhibition ever at the time, covering an area of 216 acres. There was also an amusement park designed to rival Coney Island in the USA. It was deliberately designed to be fun as well as educational. It opened again in 1925 following lower than expected visitor numbers in 1924 and proved highly popular. Its greatest legacy of all though was Wembley Stadium, demolished in the early 21st century.

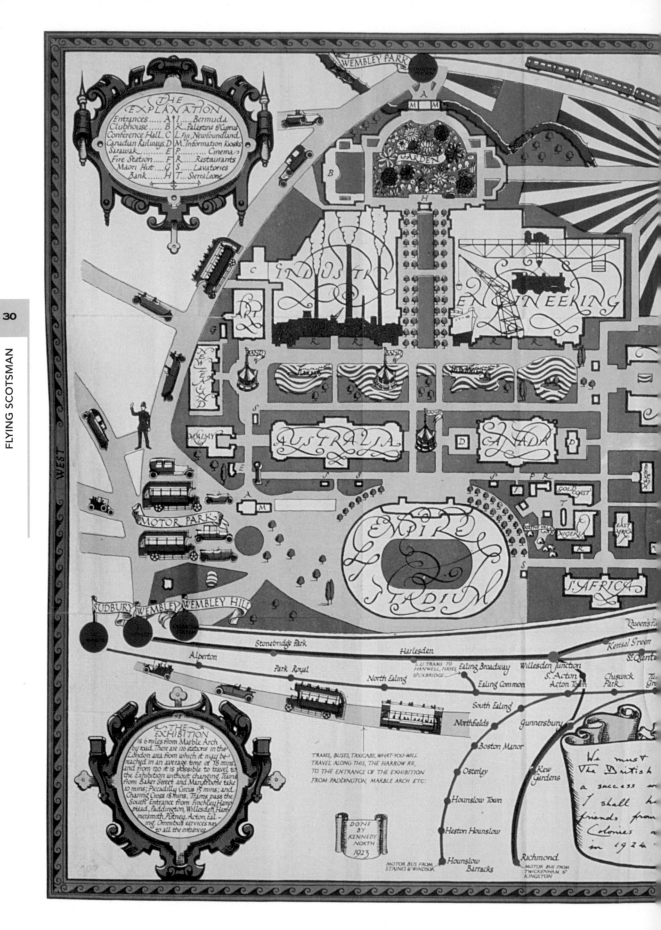

was whether the LNER could afford to take one of their latest engines out of service. Their dilemma was solved when No. 1472, the third engine in the fleet, failed severely. She faced the prospect of being out of action for some time, and was thus an ideal candidate to send to Wembley without affecting the service any more than her enforced absence already had. Then somebody within the LNER came up with a stroke of genius. The company wanted to promote itself to the public, and its most famous train was 'The Flying Scotsman'. 'The Flying Scotsman', being a train that could be formed of any locomotive and coaches if needs be, clearly couldn't be there – but what if they named No. 1472 *after the train*? At a stroke, the LNER transformed 'The Flying Scotsman' from a column in the timetable into living metal. That metal would promote the company, promote the train and, crucially, provide an evocative, resounding name. From this point on, No. 1472 ceased to be a regular locomotive: she became a legend. However,

Below Although the 'A1s' were amongst the biggest locomotives in Britain at the time, the Great Western Railway (GWR) claimed its 'Castle' 4-6-0s were more powerful, despite being smaller. A locomotive exchange between the GWR and LNER showed that the 'Castles' were significantly more efficient than the 'A1s' and this prompted Gresley to develop his 'Pacific' further. In 1925 No. 4079 *Pendennis Castle* departs London King's Cross with the 13:30 express to Leeds and Bradford.

Opposite An official side-on view of the first 'Castle' No. 4073 *Caerphilly Castle*. Like the 'A1s' the 'Castles' were supremely elegant and effective express passenger locomotives that had long careers.

it's not entirely clear where the name came from. It's known that in the nineteenth century the train that bore the official title of the 'Special Scotch Express' was very quickly nick-named 'The Flying Scotsman', and this most likely referred to its relative speed. The 'Special Scotch Express' was renamed, and No. 4472 (as she was renumbered at the end of 1923) was given appropriate nameplates.

She was repainted at Doncaster in a high gloss, varnished, beautiful apple green, which Gresley despised. He ordered that it should be 'flatted down', but happily, for once, his orders seem to have been ignored. Packed in a special wrapping, she was sent to Wembley in her full glory. She was ready to take the plaudits her builders felt she deserved. They weren't disappointed by *Flying Scotsman's* reception: she looked spectacular, and, though she remained static, she was fitted with a hidden electric motor driving her huge wheels and motion. She was one of the exhibition's star attractions. How many boys, on seeing this sparkling, apple-green colossus, decided there and then that they wanted to be engine drivers? It must have been thousands – among them, a four-year-old boy from a wealthy family in Retford, called Alan Pegler.

If the LNER was pleased with the public acclaim given to *Flying Scotsman*, it was far less happy with a display next to her: the GWR boldly claimed that the smaller *Caerphilly Castle* was the most powerful express passenger locomotive in the world. Surely, the visitors must have wondered, *Caerphilly Castle* couldn't be more powerful than *Flying Scotsman* – could she? The GWR argued that with a tractive effort (a theoretical measure to work out how much weight an engine could pull) of 31,500 lbs, compared with *Flying Scotsman's* 29,835 lbs, it was clear: the 'Castle' was the most powerful express passenger locomotive there was. On a strictly numerical basis, the GWR was ahead.

Eyebrows must have raised in Doncaster. With its bigger boiler, they argued, *Flying Scotsman* could keep pulling heavy loads at high speeds long after the 'Castles' had run out of steam. That, they said, was the true measure of power. So it must have surprised them when the GWR was prepared to rise to the challenge and agreed to test the 'Castle' head-to-head with Gresley's flagship design.

With more 'A1s' coming on stream, the LNER had enough in traffic in 1925 to agree to a series of trials with a 'Castle' on its lines; in return, an 'A1' would go to the GWR to see how Gresley's design performed on a different route. There is no definitive answer as to which side originated the trial. It has been suggested that the GWR offered the trial as a kind of bet, knowing that Gresley, with his fiercely competitive nature, would be unable to resist. But it's also entirely possible that Gresley requested the trial himself in a spirit of honest engineering inquiry: if the GWR's claims for the 'Castles' were true, there might be something to learn from it. We have already seen Gresley's willingness to learn

from others' experience, so it seems likely that the request to compare a 'Castle' with an 'A1' was about engineering rather than point-scoring.

In April 1925 the GWR sent No. 4079 *Pendennis Castle* to King's Cross shed for the first series of trials on the East Coast Main Line. She was seemingly diminutive alongside the 'A1s' at King's Cross, and onlookers must have confidently expected her to struggle with the 456-ton load as she climbed out of the station and on the greasy rails through Gasworks Tunnel on her way north. The air of anticipation must have been almost tangible. Finally, the GWR's claims of power would be shown up in the most public manner.

If they were unnerved by the doubtless partisan support for the LNER, *Pendennis Castle's* driver and fireman didn't show it. Simmering at the safety valves, the GWR locomotive awaited the guard's whistle and at its shrill blast eased her way through the tracery of pointwork outside the station without any sign of struggle or slipping: something the 'A1s' found difficult. Time and time again, *Pendennis Castle* got to grips with her heavy loads and up to speed in times that staggered even King's Cross's most ardent speed merchants. Passing times of 5 minutes 30 seconds at Finsbury Park with 330 tons were beyond reach of the 'A1s' tested in comparison. The LNER's driver was criticised for not rising to the challenge but it's unlikely this made much difference. On the LNER's home turf Gresley's 'A1s' had been found sorely wanting.

Later that year, though, the LNER sent an 'A1', No. 4474 *Victor Wild*, to Swindon for trials on the GWR, and here a very different picture emerged. Given instructions to drive

to the timetable, Driver Pibworth and his fireman swiftly got used to the Welsh coal the GWR burned, and proved that the 'A1s' were easily able to match the stiffest times set for the 'Castles'. Better still, among the steep hills of Devon, where even the 'Castles' struggled, the huge reserves of power provided by the big boiler of the 'A1' allowed her to race over them at speeds the GWR was quite unable to match with the same loads. Ultimately therefore, the trials resulted in an honourable draw, with both designs acquitting themselves well, although the coal consumption of the 'Castle' was substantially lower than Gresley's design.

Why did the smaller locomotive perform better out of King's Cross than Gresley's flagship design? The higher boiler pressure of the 'Castles' – 225psi against 180psi – made a difference, as did the way weight transferred onto the rear wheels of the locomotives on starting. Ultimately though, it was through long experimentation that the GWR had arrived at something like the ideal combination of valve and exhaust arrangements, which allowed its locomotives to use every ounce of steam. The 'A1s', with their less efficient valves, were allowing steam to leave the cylinders when it still had energy which could be used.

Impressed by the efficiency of the 'Castles' Gresley began experimenting with tweaks to the 'A1s'. First of all came changes to the valves which worked well. Then he fitted a higher pressure boiler to a pair of 'A1s'. The combination of better valves and higher pressure boiler made the locomotives more powerful but this wasn't the primary reason for ultimately modifying all the 'A1s' to this standard. The altered locomotives showed a big reduction

in the amount of coal burned and for the perennially cash-strapped LNER this was enough of an incentive to invest in the modifications. The tweaked 'A1s' were known as 'A3s' – and though nobody knew it at the time the stage was set for a period regarded to this day as a golden age for the steam railway.

Below The performance of No. 4079 *Pendennis Castle* surprised observers on the East Coast Main Line, and in May 1925 the 4-6-0 passes a goods train hauled by one of Gresley's earlier designs – a 'K3' 2-6-0 – with the 10:10 King's Cross to Leeds express.

THE GOLDEN AGE

The period from around 1925 until the Second World War was to be a high-water mark which, the critics say, has never been matched. It was a time – if you believe the publicity – when every train ran on time and was spotlessly clean, and when every passenger was served good, solid food by white-suited waiters. Britain's railways really showed their mettle during this period, led by Gresley, *Flying Scotsman* and the London and North Eastern Railway (LNER). The country depended almost totally on the railways, to a degree unknown today. Every station had a goods shed where wagons could be loaded and unloaded, and a dizzying volume of freight trains ran here, there and everywhere. Almost everything which had to be carried more than a few miles was sent by rail.

And that was just goods. The privileged few could, in theory, have driven long distances, but they didn't, because the railway was faster and the roads poor. If you wanted to travel in Britain in the 1920s and 1930s, the chances were that you went by train: there simply wasn't another option. Most people didn't need, and couldn't afford, to travel far.

It didn't stop the railways encouraging them to, though. As the 'A1s' came on stream, the LNER really got to grips with its publicity and marketing. Time and time again, the company produced promotional materials of an elegance and sophistication that takes the breath away even now. This was, in part, thanks to a recognition that of all the companies created by the Grouping, the LNER was by far the most financially fragile of the Big Four. In the absence of substance, the company would have to try to create style. While the other railways were either finding their feet or continuing pre-war style marketing, the LNER really tapped

Below The London and North Eastern Railway (LNER) wasted no time in linking *Flying Scotsman* with the service of the same name and invested in opulent carriages for her passengers. This is the Louis XVI Dining Saloon, c. 1930.

into the *zeitgeist*. This was the 1920s and the growing Art Deco school was something that, inadvertently, Gresley had anticipated with his smooth and clean design for the 'A1s'. The time was right for a marketing genius to exploit the romance of the rails. And the LNER got lucky: it had two.

The first was William Teasdale, who was the former advertising manager of the North Eastern Railway. While many railways promoted themselves with fussy, stilted, Edwardian elegance, Teasdale was different. He knew that if he could make the LNER appear glamorous, there was a good chance that the commuter crammed into his coaches on the way to London might just book holidays through the LNER rather than one of its competitors. Teasdale was extremely effective, separating the advertising department from what would now be called public relations and centralising promotion and marketing over the whole company.

Throughout the LNER's existence, it operated on a highly decentralised basis, and only a handful of functions were applied across the whole company. Marketing was one of them, and it was brilliant.

Teasdale's approach went for simplicity. Rather than trying to extol every possible virtue of a resort or a service, he chose to focus on one specific aspect. A typical example was his decision to continue using the famous '*Jolly Fisherman*' poster that the Great Northern Railway (GNR) had used to promote Skegness. It was a bright image combined with a simple message, and it worked. High-profile artists were commissioned to paint posters, and very quickly the LNER's glamorous image was assured. Teasdale's decision to have a separate press office also paid dividends, and the LNER soon proved highly adept at manipulating the media to project the image of a fast, progressive railway. Teasdale left and was replaced by Cecil Dandridge in 1927.

Dandridge made few alterations to the LNER's marketing strategy, and he continued the tradition of holding open days at locations around the system. These open days were a great way of showing off the company's latest developments to areas that hadn't, and perhaps never would, get any benefit from them. They offered footplate rides, demonstrations of signalling and the latest technology, the newest coaches, and of course, the very latest locomotives were present. The public was often charged for admission, but this was offset by the fact that the proceeds went to charity, often a benevolent fund for railwaymen. They were incredibly popular, particularly with children, but also with adults.

Below right By the 1930s *Flying Scotsman* herself had been superseded by the streamlined 'A4s' – a development of the 'A1' design.

Below left Luggage label designs showcased *Flying Scotsman*.

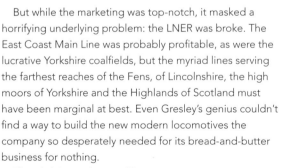

But while the marketing was top-notch, it masked a horrifying underlying problem: the LNER was broke. The East Coast Main Line was probably profitable, as were the lucrative Yorkshire coalfields, but the myriad lines serving the farthest reaches of the Fens, of Lincolnshire, the high moors of Yorkshire and the Highlands of Scotland must have been marginal at best. Even Gresley's genius couldn't find a way to build the new modern locomotives the company so desperately needed for its bread-and-butter business for nothing.

That didn't stop him and his team continuing to innovate, however. The power of the 'A1s' meant that for the first time, a railway company had a locomotive able to run over really long distances with a reasonable load. This in turn had the potential to open up new commercial opportunities and generate operational efficiencies too. The 'A1s' could haul enough coal in the tender and scoop up water at a series of troughs laid between the rails en

SKEGNESS

FRANK NEWBOULD after J. HASSALL

SKEGNESS IS SO BRACING
IT'S QUICKER BY RAIL
FREE ILLUSTRATED GUIDE FROM ANY L·N·E·R OFFICE OR AGENCY, OR DEPT. E, TOWN HALL, SKEGNESS

route, to get themselves 400 or so miles without problems. The limitation was human: to ask a driver – and, more particularly, a fireman – to work at full capacity, without a break, for up to seven hours was beyond even the working practices of the day. In fact, if done on a regular basis, it would have been downright dangerous. The question must have reverberated in Gresley's head: 'Can I change the engine crews without stopping the train?' Slowing the train down to walking pace with the new crew boarding and the old one disembarking would have been dangerous, unreliable and, if the train was moving at walking pace, pointless. Asking driver and fireman to climb over the top of the tender was equally ridiculous. In the absence of a teleporter, Gresley was stumped.

Then he had a brainwave. For years passengers had been travelling from one coach to another by corridors at the end of them. It was well established (the GNR had been one of the pioneers), so what would stop the engineers putting a corridor in the tender so that the crew could pass from the coach to the engine's cab? Providing he kept the dimensions of the corridor fairly small, he wouldn't sacrifice that much coal or water capacity, and he could always make the tender longer to compensate if needed.

Above The LNER was supremely effective at promoting the resorts it served and retained the famous 'Skegness is so Bracing' poster originally created by the Great Northern Railway (GNR) in 1908 – an image still used by the town today. The GNR paid £12 for it. This artwork was by Frank Newbould (1887–1951) after John Hassall (1868–1948), who first drew the character.

Opposite The LNER also drew on the Art Deco movement for this stunning poster. It pokes fun at a famous Southern Railway image but emphasises the power and glamour of its 'A1' and 'A3' fleets. Although spectacular, this poster was not well received by the travelling public, and was not reissued.

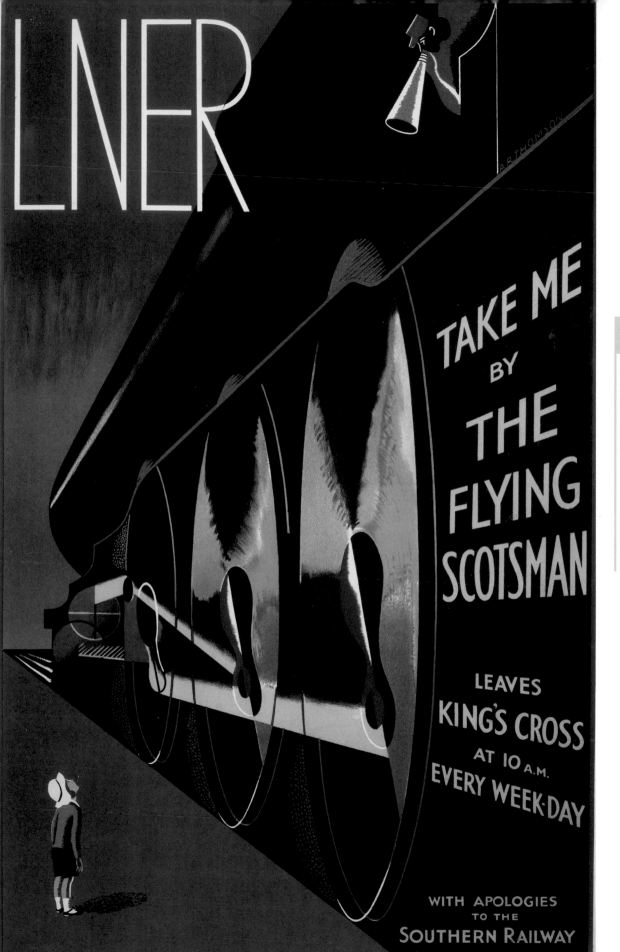

GHT SCOTSMAN"
.5 P.M.
SLEEPERS

To test his theory, he arranged an experiment in his own dining room. He laid out his chairs in the pattern he had in mind for the tender and then tried to crawl through the space; he reasoned that if a relative giant of a man like himself could get through, so could most of his crews. As he was crawling through this impromptu maze, one of his daughters walked in – one can imagine the looks that must have passed between doting father and a thoroughly confused daughter, who presumably went scurrying from the room to fetch the men in white coats. Gresley's 'Eureka' moment was a cracker, and he was allowed to perpetuate it in metal.

Secret orders were sent to the LNER's main works at Doncaster to build a tender with a corridor in it. On no account must word slip out, because Dandridge and his marketing team had come up with a plan that would guarantee headlines for days – the longest non-stop rail journey in the world – and it depended on the corridor tender. The commercial justification for this was flimsy at best, but the LNER's board was shrewd enough to know that the publicity from such a record-breaking, epoch-making run would have what would nowadays be known as a 'halo effect' on all of the LNER's other passenger services, whether justified or not. It was worth taking the risk. The LNER was going to run a train non-stop from King's Cross in London to the Scottish citadel of Edinburgh's Waverley station: a distance of 392 miles.

In great secrecy, the tender was built, and to test it, placed behind an old Ivatt 'Atlantic'. The driver was guaranteed a clear road north to Doncaster on a test train (ostensibly for braking trials) but found himself stopped at Retford. He called the signalman in a fury.

'I've got a clear road,' he must have said: 'What's going on?'

'Oh, you've got a clear road,' the signalman said. 'I stopped you because I wanted to see this new corridor tender.'

left Overnight 'sleeper' services were wide-ranging and well used in the 1930s and the LNER was no exception. This 'Scotland by the Night Scotsman' poster promoted the LNER's Anglo-Scottish overnight train with a stylised 'A1'. The big 'Pacifics' were well able to haul these heavy trains, albeit at slower speeds than the daytime expresses. The poster shows a locomotive travelling along the tracks at night. Artwork by Robert Bartlett.

Left Gresley's corridor tender allowed the LNER to run non-stop from London to Edinburgh, changing crews en route. The 392-mile distance was the longest non-stop, steam-hauled train in the world at the time.

Below The corridor at the rear of the tender linked with the leading carriage of the train and allowed a replacement crew to enter the footplate. It ran down the side of the tender, and light was provided by the circular porthole. Here *Flying Scotsman* is being prepared for her historic, non-stop run in May 1928.

Opposite The words 'Flying Scotsman' are being painted on the roof of one of the train's carriages, 1932. This was for a Marconi radio test where passengers on the train communicated with the passengers on a plane. To enable the plane to spot the train the words were painted on the rear carriage – otherwise, identifying it from the air amongst the other expresses on the East Coast Main Line would have been difficult, if not impossible.

Trials successful, the game was on. There were, though, a couple of minor problems with *Flying Scotsman* that would prevent it getting much farther north than Newcastle. The most critical was that, even though *Flying Scotsman* was a shrunk-down version of an American design, she was still too tall for some of the bridges on the former North British route from Newcastle to Edinburgh, and the platform edges at Newcastle Central station were awfully close to being hit by the 'A1s', even at low speed. Gresley cut down the height of the locomotive's chimney, boiler dome and cab to ensure she wouldn't knock any bits off. To save potential embarrassment at Newcastle, a small section of plate just below the buffers was cut away, and no more was heard from the civil engineers about it.

The press was made discreetly aware of the run, and *Flying Scotsman* was specially transferred from Doncaster to King's Cross to head the first departure. The date set

was 1 May 1928, May Day, and on an otherwise unassuming Tuesday, King's Cross station was thronged with dignitaries, reporters, well-wishers, enthusiasts, passengers and railwaymen eager to see history made.

Flying Scotsman's driver that day was Albert Pibworth, the same man who had shown such mettle during the locomotive exchanges on the Great Western Railway (GWR) during 1925. At 11:00 that morning, *Flying Scotsman* sallied forth on her way north and into the history books. Never before had anything like this been attempted, yet here was the LNER not only going for it, but on a regular basis, and in both directions, for at the same time, an identical train hauled by No. 2850 *Shotover* eased its way east out of Edinburgh Waverley on a non-stop run to London.

Flying Scotsman's journey was scheduled to take 8 hours 15 minutes, which – because of agreements between the rival East and West Coast alliances of pre-Grouping days following the races to the north – was the same as the stopping time, and at Tollerton, just north of York, Pibworth was relieved by his Gateshead counterpart Tommy Blades for the final run to Edinburgh. Crowds thronged the line-side, and as *Flying Scotsman* got closer to Edinburgh, it was clear that she still had plenty in hand. Without even trying, Blades managed to get *Flying Scotsman* and her train into Waverley station 12 minutes early. The plaudits were showered on *Flying Scotsman* and her designer – whatever the future was to hold, both were now certain of their place in the history books.

The non-stop run is crucial, not just in the story of *Flying Scotsman* and Nigel Gresley, but in the development of passenger trains too. Until then, nobody had even thought to try running such long distances non-stop: by today's standards, even most express trains were horribly slow, and, while *Flying Scotsman's* non-stop run was in one sense pointless, as it was no faster than the usual service with stops at major stations, it pointed the way forward powerfully. It was clear that the timings between London and Scotland were artificially slow, thanks to the new generation of rolling stock being introduced.

The *Flying Scotsman* ran non-stop between London and Edinburgh for the summer of 1928, reverting to its usual pattern in the winter timetable. The following year, in the summer, the non-stop service restarted with a blitz of publicity. The 'A1s' and their more powerful counterparts the 'A3s' were dominating East Coast Main Line services,

and though the GWR continued to claim dominance in the power stakes, thanks to an enlarged design of 'Castle' known as the 'Kings', in truth, there was nothing on the rails in Britain which could match the performance of Gresley's thoroughbreds on a daily basis. Gresley and his team were approaching the pinnacle of their genius.

By 1929 the GWR was sitting back in terms of locomotive innovation, content in the knowledge that its fleet would do all the work needed of it for a generation to come, and that only replacements for worn-out and life-expired rolling stock were needed. The Southern Railway was beginning an extensive electrification programme, and, by and large, its steam developments were seen as stopgaps; and the London, Midland & Scottish Railway (LMS) was only just beginning to find its feet after a tumultuous period of reorganisation. Only Gresley and the LNER had any mind

Below In the late 1930s *Flying Scotsman* lost her corridor tender as more powerful locomotives came on stream, but even with a GNR tender she epitomises the spectacle of the railways of the period. In 1938 the locomotive passes Ganwick with a King's Cross to Peterborough semi-fast train.

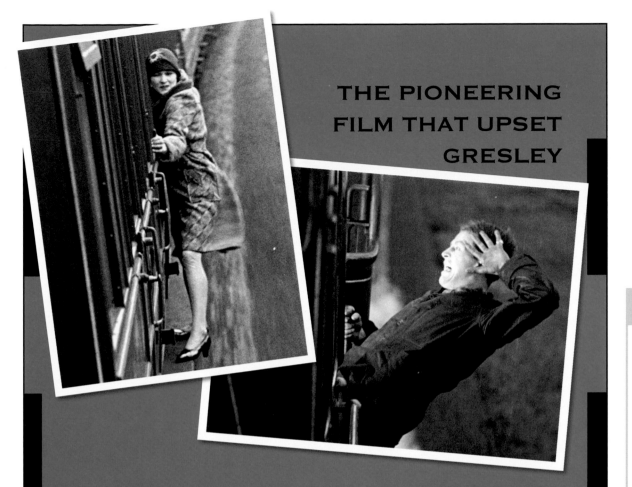

THE PIONEERING FILM THAT UPSET GRESLEY

Flying Scotsman starred in the pioneering 1929 film *The Flying Scotsman*, widely regarded as either the first or second British film to use sound. The plot follows a bid for revenge by No. 4472's former fireman, who had been dismissed for drinking at work after being reported by the engine's driver, Bob. On Bob's last day working on *Flying Scotsman* the fireman decides to take action. The replacement fireman has unknowingly fallen in love with a girl – Bob's daughter – who tries to stop the villain. The film was shot on the Hertford loop and was notable for some of its stunts, including when the lead actress Pauline Johnson, climbs out of the coaches and along the outside of the train at speed to access the locomotive. Shot in real time the stunt was extremely dangerous. LNER Chief Mechanical Engineer Nigel Gresley was appalled at unsafe practices shown in the film and insisted on a declaimer in the opening credits aimed at reassuring the travelling public that such events would never happen on the LNER.

Reise bequem!

BILDER
VOM PERSONENVERKEHR
DER DEUTSCHEN REICHSBAHN

to continue developing the steam locomotive, though one could argue convincingly that, such was the performance of the 'A1s' and 'A3s', all that was needed was a freight locomotive using the same boiler and a really useful mixed-traffic design along the lines of the GWR's 'Hall' class.

Gresley had other ideas and wanted to explore the possibilities of using marine-type boilers on a steam locomotive. On many ships, boilers worked at a much higher pressure and then used the exhaust steam from one high-pressure cylinder to drive larger but lower-pressure cylinders in a process known as compounding. They were much more efficient than the simple-expansion process used in most steam locomotives, but also more complicated. There had been some successful compound designs in Britain, but most had been found wanting. Gresley thought he could make it work in a large express locomotive, and prepared designs for a radical new engine to be built at Darlington. In December 1929, he introduced, with great fanfare, No. 10000. This streamlined giant of a locomotive – bigger than *Flying Scotsman* – was painted battleship grey and looked like nothing else on the rails before or since. Gresley's aim had been to reduce coal

Opposite Germany led the way in seeking alternatives to steam traction in the 1930s and promoted its own scenic railways heavily during this period.

Below The diesel-powered 'Flying Hamburger' train was a genuine revolution, establishing principles which are still in use today. The LNER investigated a development of it for the East Coast Main Line but concluded that its performance could be matched by the 'A1s' and 'A3s' with a light load – and without the catering limitations of the diesel trains.

consumption, but, although No. 10000 proved extremely powerful, she was also a hungry and unreliable performer.

The 1929 Wall Street crash hit the LNER hard, decimating much of its traffic, and in a bid to keep costs down, jobs were cut and strict limits imposed on overtime. It wasn't unusual either for huge numbers of trains to be cancelled in order to save coal: funds really were that tight.

Yet ironically, with Gresley's powerful 'Pacific' locomotives, the LNER was able, potentially, to offer a more attractive long-distance passenger service than ever before. Eventually, patience with the artificially low London to Edinburgh travel time of 8 hours and 30 minutes ran out, and in May 1932 it was cut by 45 minutes. Speed was starting to become important again – and not just in Britain.

The problems of Germany in the 1920s and 1930s are well-documented: hyperinflation, high unemployment and rampant fascism. It wasn't until the 1930s that the country started to get on its feet again, and the price it paid for that was Hitler. The nationalised railway, Deutsche Reichsbahn, was among the most innovative in the world, and the Germans were amongst the first adopters of electric trains in regular service. Spurred on by heavy government investment, Deutsche Reichsbahn started developing high-speed trains using alternatives to steam. Eventually the investment paid off, and in 1932 the Germans were able to announce that a new design of diesel train had hit 124mph on test – and that they hoped to introduce it into revenue-earning service the following year.

This design, which became known as the 'Flying Hamburger', offered a compelling and prophetic vision of the future of rail travel: it had no separate locomotive, relying instead on small but powerful diesel engines under the floor. These drove a generator to supply power to the electric motors which, in turn, drove the wheels; a new signalling system would apply brakes if the train exceeded the speed limit or passed a red signal. This articulated, two-car train was the weapon Deutsche Reichsbahn intended to use to fight the increasingly popular airlines on the crucial Berlin–Hamburg corridor. With a top speed of 100mph it was easily able to reach in service, the 'Flying Hamburger' was able to average 77mph consistently for the 178-mile journey. This was the future, and it had a massive impact.

Diesel trains offered a number of advantages over steam. They were cleaner and, because they didn't need smoke-boxes emptying every day and water filling up throughout, were able to work longer between servicing. They were potentially faster and only needed one man on the footplate, rather than the driver and fireman that a steam locomotive required.

Most of the early diesel trains had just one or two coaches, but the LNER, always keen to save money, was sufficiently intrigued by the 'Flying Hamburger' to send Gresley's assistant, Oliver Bulleid, over to Germany to take a look at it. Bulleid was impressed with the smoothness and speed of the German train, though he noted that it had suffered teething troubles. His report encouraged Gresley

to take a look for himself, and Gresley immediately recognised that this train, or something like it, could revolutionise express passenger travel on the LNER. On his return, he asked the Germans to provide a detailed estimate for the LNER board of the impact of running a three-coach, 'Flying Hamburger' train between London and Newcastle, working to a 4-hour schedule.

The Germans were scrupulously honest. The 'Flying Hamburger' couldn't, they said, do better than 4½ hours between King's Cross and Newcastle. Even worse, because offering hot meals on the train would have been extremely difficult, due to space problems, the best that could be offered in terms of catering was a cold buffet service of the type popular in Germany. That, of course, wouldn't be nearly enough for diners more used to proper cooked meals with roast potatoes and Yorkshire puddings. It would have been a compromise too far for the LNER.

With further development, it is fairly certain that a diesel train akin to the Flying Hamburger could have matched the LNER's needs, but already Gresley was thinking along different lines. He reasoned that diesel trains were expensive to buy and maintain, and in the 1930s their efficiency gains over steam were not that great. Furthermore, he knew that with a light load of something like 250 tons, some types of steam locomotives were quite capable of very high average speeds over long distances.

Though there was some concern at board level about the state of the track in areas of extensive coal mining, Gresley was able to persuade the directors to allow some high-speed tests using an ordinary locomotive and carriages. It was planned to run with three coaches – a first-class corridor coach, a first-class and dining car and a kitchen car – and to this short rake would be added a dynamometer car: a coach fitted with sensitive measuring equipment that would be able to accurately record speed and location information. The load behind the locomotive would be something like 147 tons: a mere trifle. The plan was to run between King's Cross and Leeds in 2 hours 45 minutes each way: an average speed of 67.5mph.

To emphasise that standard equipment was being used, it was decided to use one of the early 'A1' 4-6-2s, rather than the uprated 'A3s'. Of these, the LNER opted for No. 4472 *Flying Scotsman*, the company's flagship – though not, it must be said, the best of the fleet by any means. King's

Below *Flying Scotsman* was the first steam locomotive to verifiably reach 100mph, and in 1935 her classmate, No. 2750 *Papyrus*, showed how fast and free-running the 'A3s' were by reaching 108mph – a world record – on 5 March 1935. This is an official works photograph of the locomotive at Doncaster.

Cross driver William Sparshatt was chosen to drive the train because of his reputation as something of a speed merchant. Considerations of coal consumption simply didn't apply to him – he was definitely the right man for the job!

On 30 November 1934 *Flying Scotsman* flew out of King's Cross on her way north to Leeds. Sparshatt left observers in no doubt about the capabilities of *Flying Scotsman*. She charged the step gradient of Stoke Bank near Grantham recording a minimum speed of 81mph, having already hit 94.75mph on the descent from Stevenage. Sparshatt arrived in Leeds 13 minutes ahead of the schedule, in 151 minutes, and at an average speed of 73.4mph.

The northward run was so good that it was decided to add an extra couple of coaches for the return journey to London, taking the weight up to 207.5 tons. This time *Flying Scotsman* would have Stoke Bank, one of the greatest racing stretches of line anywhere in Britain, to hare down. First though, she had to climb five miles uphill at 1:200 from Grantham to reach the summit. Sparshatt had the bit between his teeth and thrashed *Flying Scotsman* uphill. Her chimney barked her exhaust note in blocks of furious defiance at this treatment, her fireman flung coal desperately into the firebox to keep the steam rate up, and finally she crested the summit of Stoke Bank at 68.5mph and got her nose down. The speed started rising on this magical stretch of line and *Flying Scotsman* continued to accelerate towards the little station of Essendine. Just before she was compelled to slow down, the dynamometer car peaked at 100mph: the first time this had been verifiably recorded by a steam locomotive anywhere in the world. Undaunted, Sparshatt thrashed *Flying Scotsman* onward, racing her into King's Cross in a time of 157 minutes 17 seconds. It was a new record from Leeds to London and an amazing performance from driver, fireman and locomotive. It was starting to look as if Gresley's belief that steam power could match the diesels might just be true.

The following year plans were put in hand for a test using one of the more powerful 'A3' 4-6-2s, No. 2750 *Papyrus*, this time to Newcastle. She averaged 68mph, recording a maximum of 88.5mph on the northbound run – proof that an 'A3' could run at high speeds for long periods. For the return, it was a slightly different story. This time, with Sparshatt again at the regulator, an official speed record attempt would be made on Stoke Bank. It surprised no one that between Doncaster and Grantham, Sparshatt nursed

left Although the 'A3s' were brilliant machines Gresley continued development of new types. Although the 'P2' 2-8-2s were not replicated widely, they prompted him to experiment with streamlining, ultimately used to brilliant effect on the 'A4' 4-6-2s. Here the first 'P2', No. 2001, *Cock o' the North*, approaches Welwyn Garden City in Hertfordshire, on her way to King's Cross on 11 June 1934.

his charge, giving his fireman time to build up a really big, hot fire. *Papyrus* hit the summit of Stoke Bank at the same speed as *Flying Scotsman*, but from then on, the newer locomotive's better valves and higher boiler pressure started to tell. As she passed Little Bytham, 8 miles downhill from the summit of Stoke Bank, she was averaging 96.9mph, and then went faster still on the 1:200 descent from there, hitting a record 108mph. She arrived in King's Cross in 23 minutes – well under the 9½ hours the Germans promised from the 'Flying Hamburger' on the same route. *Papyrus* hadn't just beaten her sister's record: she'd smashed the unverified claims of competitors from Europe and America too. Gresley's 'Pacifics' were the fastest steam locomotives in the world. With the argument about whether steam could match newer technology well and truly sorted, Gresley turned his attention to designing a locomotive that could achieve the high averages of *Flying Scotsman* and *Papyrus* without overworking the fireman. He had built a new locomotive called *Cock o' the North*, ostensibly for operation on the tough line between Edinburgh and Aberdeen. In truth, however, this machine was to be a guinea pig to test new ideas on. She had a wedge-shaped front and smoothed sides to reduce air resistance. She had a big boiler and a 2-8-2 wheel arrangement, so she had more grip than an 'A1' or 'A3'. Gresley had high hopes and sent her over to the French test facility at Vitry to be evaluated scientifically. The news wasn't good, though: she was heavy on coal and her wheel bearings were prone to overheating.

For Gresley it was something of a disappointment, but he wasn't deterred – he decided instead to develop the 'A3', as *Papyrus* had shown that the fundamentals of the design were well able to cope with high speeds. What he had in mind was something akin to an 'A3' GT. Its fundamentals would be based on the older design, but improved: the boiler would be of 250psi instead of 220, the cylinders would have a different bore, and all the internal pipes that carried steam and water would be made as gently curved as possible to minimise resistance. The crowning glory would be an all-new, streamlined casing similar in concept to that of No. 10000.

It took much experimentation in a wind tunnel to get the shape right, and it was with some trepidation that Gresley presented his proposals for a streamlined train to run between London and Newcastle, timed to coincide with the twenty-fifth anniversary of King George V's accession to the throne. It would be called, with prescient timing, the Silver Jubilee.

The board took its time considering Gresley's plans: it would cost a lot of money, but it might be worth it if the service proved a success. They gave the project the green light on the understanding that it would enter service on 30 September 1935. There was precious little time.

Four streamlined 'A3' GTs were to be built, given the classification 'A4'. They would haul a new set of luxury coaches incorporating the latest developments, such as air-conditioning, an electric kitchen and separate restaurant cars for first- and second-class. In recognition of the Silver Jubilee theme, each locomotive's name would start with 'Silver', and both engine and coaches would be painted in a mixture of subtle greys.

The frames for the first locomotive, *Silver Link*, were laid on 26 June 1935, and less than a month later, she left Doncaster Works for trials. She was an absolute sensation. With her wedge-shaped streamlined front, she looked nothing like anything else on the rails, and her silver-grey colour scheme shone brilliantly amongst the apple green of the other passenger locomotives.

Three days before the public launch, a demonstration trip for press and invited guests was held. Though LNER chairman Sir Ralph Wedgwood said no record attempt would be made, vases of cut flowers on the tables were removed by stewards before she set off. She was quickly up to speed and hared through Hitchin at 107mph. Soon afterwards Gresley himself was reluctantly forced to go through the corridor tender to tell the crew to slow down: 'Ease your arm young man,' he told driver Taylor. 'We have twice touched 112mph!' Taylor said he thought the train had only been travelling at around 90mph, so smooth was the ride, and Gresley softened: 'Go a bit easier, we have an old director in the back and he's getting a bit touchy.'

Gresley's 'A4' 4-6-2 – the ultimate development of *Flying Scotsman* – was a massive success, and now that they had a locomotive able to run really fast, the LNER wasted little time in reaping the marketing benefits. Two more streamlined trains were put into service: the 'Coronation', from London to Edinburgh, and the 'West Riding Limited', which ran from London to Leeds and Bradford. For *Flying Scotsman*, it marked the end of her career at the top of the locomotive league table. She was already outclassed by her close relations, the 'A3s', and the advent of the 'A4' meant *Flying Scotsman* was relegated to lesser duties, though always on the East Coast Main Line, and always on passenger trains.

Opposite For all their streamlined casing the 'A4s' were, under the skin, a logical development of the 'A3s'. The LNER rolled out streamlined trains on key routes and the 'West Riding Limited' served Bradford and Leeds from London. The heavily stylised 'A4' in this 1938 poster certainly conveys the appearance – but purists might suggest an accurate reproduction of the 'A4' would have looked even better. Artwork by Charles 'Shep' Shepherd, who studied art under Paul Woodroffe and was head of the studio at the Baynard Press. He designed posters for the Royal Mail Packet Steam Company and London Transport as well as Southern Railway.

"WEST RIDING
LIMITED"
THE FIRST STREAMLINE TRAIN
BRADFORD LEEDS LONDON
KING'S CROSS
WINTER 1938-39
LONDON & NORTH EASTERN RAILWAY

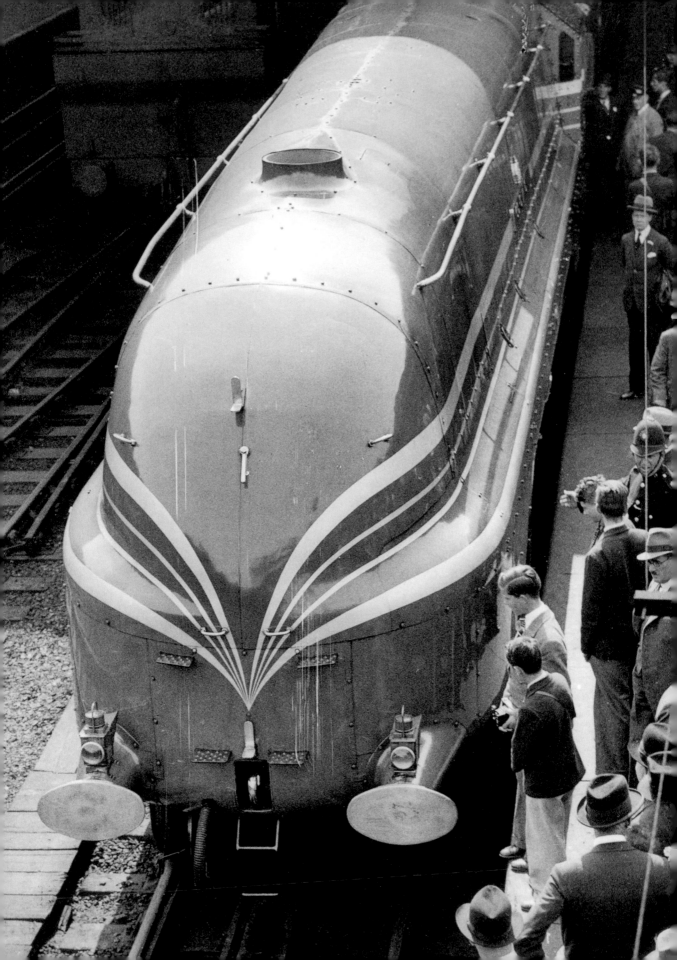

Flying Scotsman, still in her original form, finally lost her corridor tender in October 1936 as more 'A4s' came on stream. For eight years, she had been one of the flagship long-distance locomotives of the LNER, and though she wouldn't be asked to run such long distances non-stop, she remained a vital part of the front-line fleet at King's Cross. Life as a fleet engine was slightly different from the pampered-racehorse regime applied to the non-stop and streamlined trains. Those machines were given special attention at the engine sheds to ensure they were in tip-top condition: a failure on the 'Silver Jubilee' simply wouldn't do. It meant that *Flying Scotsman* and the other 'A1s' received a very slightly lower standard of maintenance, in recognition that their duties weren't now as demanding as they once were.

The LNER's speed records were quickly beaten, first by the LMS and then by the Germans, who hit 124.5mph. Gresley wanted to see how fast his streamlined 'A4s' could go, and on 3 July 1938, No. 4468 *Mallard* set an all-time record for steam of 126mph. The morale boost for the LNER, and indeed for Britain, was significant, but it made little difference to the day-to-day operation of the railways: the staff had enough on their plates with the day jobs.

It was the high-water mark for steam. Streamlined, advanced locomotives were hauling equally beautiful trains that exuded an air of glamour and style not seen since. Even if one had to travel daily on packed and filthy commuter trains, the sight of one of these trains passing by couldn't have failed to evoke an emotion similar to that of seeing Concorde when it was in service. And the LNER had such panache: whether it was the streamlined 'A4s' or the graceful and elegant 'A1s' and 'A3s', its front-line locomotive fleet epitomised the Art Deco ideals of cleanliness in design and pride in appearance. It may well have been a triumph of style over substance, but the LNER, and to a lesser extent the LMS and Great Western, have given us a compelling cultural memory of a gentler, more civilised and glamorous way of travelling. It truly was a golden era, and it was soon to come crashing down with the Second World War.

left It wasn't just the LNER which ran streamlined trains – its great rival the London Midland and Scottish Railway developed the 'Princess Coronation' 4-6-2s for its 'Coronation Scot' train from London Euston to Glasgow in a bid to compete with the LNER. This photograph shows the scene just before departure of the train on 23 June 1937.

END OF AN ERA

resley died in April 1941, ill and exhausted. But he could look back at a career that from gentle beginnings at the London and North Western Railway had taken him into the pantheon of engineering greats, along with the likes of Brunel, Stephenson and Churchward. His locomotives and carriages had set standards that would remain unbeaten for decades.

But the world had changed massively since the formation of the London and North Eastern Railway (LNER) in 1923. Then, big, complicated express locomotives and trains could be justified on the grounds of prestige and the availability of cheap, plentiful labour to staff, maintain and service them. But in 1941 Britain's ability to sustain its struggle against Germany was being tested to the limit, thanks to the depredations of the U-boats, and those big, complicated express locomotives and luxury trains were starting to look rather redundant at a time when Britain needed every locomotive, carriage and wagon in service to help the war effort. All four railway companies were in a more or less similar situation – too many locomotives requiring too much maintenance at a time when the nation

could least afford it – but the LNER was probably in a worse situation than the others, not helped by its lack of cash.

It was a difficult time for the railways, as it was for everyone else. The war effort took priority over all other traffic, and even the railways were denuded of all but the bare minimum of support staff. On the outbreak of

Below The Second World War ended the so-called golden age of the steam railway for good. Railways and workers were in the front line and crews were issued with gas masks for use during air raids. Here the driver is on Great Western Railway 'Castle' No. 5085 *Evesham Abbey* – but all railway workers were at risk of air attack.

Opposite Under government control the railways issued a series of posters promoting their importance to the war effort. Many railway staff were exempted from military service so vital were their skills. Despite extended journey times and a rail network busier than ever passenger numbers soared, in part due to the vast numbers of military personnel travelling around the country.

A MIGHTY WAR EFFORT

Railways are vital
FOR
DEFENCE NEEDS
FOOD DISTRIBUTION
PUBLIC TRANSPORT

ISSUED BY THE RAILWAY EXECUTIVE COMMITTEE

WATERLOW & SONS LTD LONDON & DUNSTABLE.

Above A woman waves goodbye to soldiers off to war on 9 November 1939. They were being sent to join the British Expeditionary Force in France, but would soon return after the Dunkirk evacuation the following year. At the outbreak of war all of Britain's private railways were taken under government control for the duration.

war, the government took control of the railways for the duration, and almost immediately many locomotives were painted black to help camouflage them. The apple-green express livery of the LNER was simply too visible from the air, particularly at night. This simple move immediately emphasised the urgency of the situation and, combined with the blackout, meant that pre-war glamour had given way to outright practicality. The streamlined trains so popular before the war were now essentially useless, and the carriages were stored, as was much of the 'A4' locomotive fleet for a while.

nameboards removed in a bid to thwart German spies, such were the security concerns at the time. But this was only the beginning of the difficulties: with so many military personnel travelling all over the country, passenger trains were packed with people, and the chances of getting a seat were minimal.

When one considers that before the war a long passenger train might have had twelve coaches or so, the lengths of some trains during the war beggared belief. The record, it seems, goes to one of twenty-six coaches hauled out of King's Cross by a Gresley 'V2'. That was exceptional, but it certainly wasn't unknown for the locomotives on passenger trains leaving King's Cross to be in Gasworks Tunnel before departure.

For engine crews, the war brought a host of new challenges. The need to sustain the blackout meant that many locomotives had side windows plated over, and on tender engines, awkward blackout sheets were fitted, which were supposed to stretch between cab and tender (the glow of a firebox at night representing a tantalising target of opportunity for a roaming Luftwaffe pilot with bullets and bombs to spare).

Operating conditions became worse as well. Simple things like fire irons and tools became scarce, with many crews having to steal them from other locomotives. Locomotives were cleaned less frequently and were often kept in service in a condition that before the war would have seen them sent for overhaul and repair. It didn't help that parts of the main locomotive works were turned over to military production meaning that, over time, a maintenance backlog developed. On top of this, trains were often delayed by hours because of congestion and failure; crews could be on the footplate for twelve hours at a time – long enough for a non-stop run from London to Aberdeen with 1890s timings – so bad was the situation.

After Gresley's death in 1941 the LNER board appointed as his successor the man they considered best able to deliver the rolling stock the company needed at the lowest cost in capital, labour and ongoing maintenance; what was needed in wartime wasn't a brilliant vision, it was practical, down-to-earth engineering competence. The man they chose was the carriage and wagon superintendent, Edward Thompson, by now aged sixty. He was a good choice, as witnessed by his work in the carriage and wagon department, and it was a logical promotion for which he'd waited a long time. Even so, eighteen years after his father-in-law Vincent Raven had been passed over for the post of Chief Mechanical Engineer (CME) in favour of Gresley, Thompson still hadn't forgiven his predecessor.

On arrival at Doncaster, one of the first things he is reputed to have said to his senior team is: 'I have a lot to do and very little time to do it.' Clearly, things were going to change a lot. They needed to. The availability and reliability

It didn't take long for someone to recognise that storing such powerful locomotives was an act of folly. With traffic demands at a high and growing throughout the war, spare locomotives were at a premium, and if the only locomotive available for a freight train was one of Gresley's sublime 'Pacifics', so be it.

Freight and troop movements took priority over all other traffic, and this, combined with a maximum speed limit of 60mph imposed on all passenger trains, meant that for those civilian passengers who had to travel journeys became much harder. Many stations had their

of Gresley's big express locomotives, the 'V2s', the 'A1' and 'A3' 4-6-2s, and the streamlined 'A4s', was by now starting to become a major concern. All four designs were performing prodigious feats, hauling trains of lengths and weights far beyond anything Gresley could have imagined, but they were failing too often. Thompson laid the blame for this squarely on the conjugated valve gear so beloved of Gresley. He was probably right to.

Though certain railway occupations, such as engine crew and many engineering roles, were exempt from conscription (they were known as reserved occupations), other jobs, such as cleaning, invariably fell by the wayside

owing to staff shortages and the rush to get engines into service. For the conjugated valve gear, this lack of cleaning proved little short of disastrous. Gresley had placed its levers in front of the cylinders to make maintenance and adjustment easier, but there was a catch: the assembly was vulnerable to fine and gritty smokebox ash falling out of the front of the locomotive during routine maintenance. If any that landed on the plating in front of the smokebox wasn't cleaned off thoroughly after the smokebox was emptied, it could find its way everywhere, including into the precisely installed motion that drove the valves for the middle cylinder of the conjugated valve gear.

These sharp particles increased the wear on the valve gear, and the lack of regular tender loving care in the running sheds only exacerbated the problem. Something, felt Thompson, needed to be done. There were sceptics about his view even in 1941, but it's difficult to see what choice he really had at the time. The conjugated valve gear was a major cause for operational concern, and action needed to be taken to improve it.

While he was considering his options on this, Thompson was also preparing a 'go-anywhere' mixed-traffic locomotive design along the lines of similar types introduced by the other 'Big Four' companies. Efficiency

Above After Gresley's death in 1941, his successor Edward Thompson took a simpler view of locomotive design, aiming at reliability and ease of maintenance. His best design was the versatile 'B1' 4-6-0, which was able to haul everything from slow goods to express passenger traffic. In this 1956 image, No. 61364 – now under British Railways (BR) ownership – pilots 'L1' 2-6-4T past Potters Bar with a suburban passenger train.

in operation and maintenance were paramount: aesthetics and speed would have to come second if necessary. Thompson's first design, the 'B1' 4-6-0, was an instant hit, proving itself both powerful and fast. It was built into the 1950s, and was one of the last steam types to remain in service, running until 1967.

It took time for Thompson to decide what to do about the conjugated valve gear, and, with victory looming from about 1943 (not to mention an influx of cheaply built heavy freight locomotives from the USA and Britain's own independent locomotive builders reducing the need to run passenger locomotives on unsuitable duties), he started to consider what the next generation of express passenger locomotives should be. Under his new philosophy, maximum use would be made of standard components,

such as connecting rods, with little room for variation.

Thompson, like many engineers, preferred to split the load of the cylinders, with the outside pair driving on to the middle coupled axle, and the middle cylinder driving on the leading coupled axle. This design, known as divided drive, reduced the stress imposed on the middle crank axle, and would have no effect on the amount of grip a locomotive could exert. However, Thompson's policy of conformity meant that he decided to move the inside cylinder forward and provide a separate set of valve gear for it. This would make maintenance more time-consuming but simpler, and so would increase reliability.

Of course, he had to prove his theory, and funds were too tight to allow him to do it with a new locomotive; he would have to rebuild first. He started in 1943 with the graceful

Below After Thompson retired in 1946, Arthur Peppercorn took over and introduced the last generation of East Coast Main Line steam locomotives. The 'A1' 4-6-2s were the spiritual successors to *Flying Scotsman* and were immensely powerful and reliable. None were saved for preservation but in 2008 a replica, No. 60163 *Tornado* was steamed and runs to this day on the National Rail network. The steams through Rewe with the 'Torbay Express', a regular charter train to Paignton.

Right Arthur Peppercorn's designs came just before nationalisation but the remainder of the orders were built by BR.

and elegant 'P2' 2-8-2s used on the onerous Edinburgh to Aberdeen run. These beautiful machines were converted into ungainly 'Pacifics' that simply looked wrong. Moving the middle cylinder forward forced Thompson to stretch the front end, and the location of the new bogie saw the outside cylinders look much further backwards than on Gresley's designs. Then he went further still, converting a quartet of the magnificent 'V2' 2-6-2s on the production line into an even odder-looking bunch of locomotives. With their smaller boilers, they looked as if the builders had run short of metal.

Thompson by now had the bit well and truly between his teeth, and wanted to convert an 'A1' into one of his new 'standard' 4 6-2s to showcase his design. He could have chosen any of eighteen locomotives for this (including *Flying Scotsman*). Yet, in an act of calculated destruction, he chose the pioneer of them all, *Great Northern* herself.

She emerged from works in September 1945, and the shockwaves can still be felt if you look at a picture. Gone was the neat layout of yore, with curved splashers covering the tops of the wheels and the outside cylinders nesting neatly halfway between the wheels of the front bogie. With her cylinders set well back, and the smokebox extended, she looked almost as if the front end of a different engine had been bolted on to her. In some senses, it had been. Going back, the extension of the cab sidesheets to meet the bottom of the firebox and tender was gone, leaving it perched precariously, the critics argued. It's ironic, and possibly deliberate, that these rebuilds looked so ugly compared with Thompson's 'B1' design. His desire, nurtured for years, to eliminate Gresley's legacy was nothing short of outright desecration.

If *Great Northern's* performances had been transformed to, say, the levels reached by the 'A4' fleet in tip-top condition, but with greater reliability, then Thompson's rebuilding might have been defensible. It wasn't. *Great Northern*, like all of Thompson's rebuilds, failed to get close to the performances recorded by the 'A3s' and 'A4s', and didn't offer good enough reliability to compensate. It is no coincidence that of all the LNER's 'Pacifics', it was Thompson's which were withdrawn first. Thankfully, Thompson's ability to inflict further damage on the 'Pacific' fleet was limited by his retirement in 1946. *Flying Scotsman* remained intact as an 'A1', while Thompson's successor, Arthur Peppercorn, set about trying to limit the damage.

In 1946 *Flying Scotsman* was roughly halfway through her life, and still in her original form. Her once record-breaking performance was now regarded as everyday, and she was just another member of the largest stable of 'Pacifics' in Britain. After the trauma of Thompson, his successor was preparing designs for what he intended to be the final generation of express steam locomotives on the East Coast Main Line before the introduction of a fleet of diesel locomotives, and then eventual electrification.

Peppercorn, a heart-and-soul Great Northern man, agreed with Thompson about splitting the drive between the leading and middle coupled axle, but he disagreed profoundly about having to have all the coupling rods of the same length. By using shorter components than for the outside cylinders, he was able to eliminate the need to lengthen the locomotives, benefiting their appearance.

At a time when the Doncaster design staff was already expressing concern about Thompson's front-end design, Peppercorn must have been welcomed with sighs of relief. In 1947 Gresley's 'A1' design was reclassified 'A10'. Peppercorn's 'A1' design was entirely new and perhaps the most modern in the country at the time. Thompson's final 'Pacific' design, the 'A2', was revised in the light of Peppercorn's and Doncaster preferences, and eventually became extremely successful. Peppercorn's 'A1' was a true successor to *Flying Scotsman* and her brethren. Fast, powerful, and exceedingly reliable, it was finally to prove to be the design that could displace many of the 'A3s' to other routes which were crying out for high-quality express passenger locomotives. The replica of this design, No. 60163 *Tornado*, was completed in 2008 and has since shown just how good Peppercorn's flagship locomotive really was to a new audience.

At the outbreak of war in 1939, the government had promised to cover the cost of rehabilitating the railways after victory, but in 1945 there was a different government with entirely different motives. Clement Attlee had been elected on a socialist mandate and promised widespread reform, from the introduction of a national health service to improved education and, crucially, nationalisation of the industries which had worked so well under government supervision (if not control) during the war. Conveniently, the 1922 Railways Act had made provision for nationalisation of the Big Four twenty-five years later – in 1948.

Initial attempts to speed up train services after the war were hit by the state of the track, which really made the high-80 and 90mph speeds of the 1930s impossible until repairs were undertaken. Even so, the LNER reintroduced many of its named trains in a bid to try to improve morale, the theory being that, even if journey times were still extraordinarily long, passengers would feel happier about the train if it was named. Whether it worked or not is unrecorded.

In 1947, almost twenty-five years after she emerged from Doncaster Works, *Flying Scotsman* was finally modified into an 'A3'. Her old 180psi boiler was replaced by a more powerful 220psi version, and her cylinders and valves were replaced with the more efficient types developed in the light of the 1925 locomotive exchange with the Great Western Railway. Now more powerful than ever, she received her final number in LNER ownership, the anonymous 103.

Below As BR ran down its steam fleet from the 1950s the locomotives took on a distinctly unkempt appearance. Nonetheless, 'A1' No. 60117 *Bois Roussel* exudes power and speed as it passes Markham. This was the final flourish of East Coast Main Line steam before diesels took over.

With the advent of nationalisation, rationalisation of Britain's railways also began. First, with the introduction of the British Railways (BR) Standard steam locomotives, there was a cull of pre-nationalisation locomotive designs, but more drastic changes were needed to keep the railway as a useful transport asset and to contend with the rapidly expanding road network.

Private car ownership was beginning to rise, and to compete with the comfort, rail had to be faster and more luxurious. BR's Mark 1 coaches began to appear from 1954, but it was 1955 that saw perhaps the most important change to the railways, in the Modernisation Plan. Under this plan BR would spend £1,240 million on new diesel locomotives to rid the network of dirty, ageing and increasingly expensive steam power. Similarly, freight traffic was being lost to the roads, and the railway needed new designs to compete with lorries.

The writing was on the wall for steam, but, thanks to a handful of dedicated and progressive staff, steam's

performances were set to get even better. The charge was led by a brilliant young shedmaster called Peter Townend, who, in 1956, became the youngest boss of King's Cross's prestigious 'Top Shed', the London home of the East Coast's stable of racehorses

Townend, born in 1925, had enjoyed a swift rise through the ranks and, after impressing his seniors with his enthusiasm and ability, landed one of the toughest tasks on the railway – sorting out the problems at Top Shed. In 1956 it's no exaggeration to say that this critical piece of the maintenance jigsaw had serious problems. Reliability of its fleet was collapsing, and there were real questions being asked of it after its usual allocation of nineteen 'A4s' and twelve 'A3s' was increased to forty-two 'Pacifics', once through working to Newcastle and Leeds was introduced (previously, engines were changed en route). There were also problems of racism, with whites and 'coloureds'

Below On 1 June 1963 Top Shed at King's Cross is quiet. On the left an 'A4' has its streamlined front end open to allow smokebox cleaning while a fitter attends to a Peppercorn 'Pacific' in the centre. On the right are two British Railways (BR) Standard '9F' 2-10-0s – the last steam locomotives built for fleet service in Britain – and although designed for heavy freight duties were well capable of speeds of up to 90mph.

Below Modifications to the 'A3s' restored them to the top table of express traction. In something approaching its final form No. 60103 *Flying Scotsman* hurries north near Huntingdon with an express from King's Cross on the evening of 9 June 1959.

Opposite *Flying Scotsman* emerges from Welwyn North Tunnel on 20 July 1959. The graffiti refers to the impending modernisation of the railways – but while enthusiasts mourned the demise of steam many train crew preferred the cleaner and warmer working conditions in the cabs of the diesels.

unbelievably having separate mess rooms. Townend had one hell of a challenge.

He rose to it with enthusiasm, first sorting out the bearing problems that the streamlined 'A4s' had suffered since the fleet was introduced in the 1930s. Thanks to taking a personal interest in the work being undertaken at the shed, he was able to increase the mileages being worked by the locomotives between failures from their previous low levels to some of the highest anywhere in Britain. It was a remarkable turnaround, and it continued because Townend wanted to improve the steaming of his locomotives.

In the 1950s most of the really good coal being mined in Britain was exported to earn precious foreign exchange, and that meant that industry, including the railways, had to make do with what was left. Much of this coal was pretty awful stuff, and, though the worst was reserved for freight locomotives, a lot of it didn't burn as hot as the coal the Gresley 'Pacifics' had enjoyed before the war. This meant that, in order to keep up with steam demand, more coal had to be shovelled on, adding to running costs. With a poor load of coal, even the best crews would struggle to get the most out of their charge.

But Townend, along with other colleagues on the former Great Western Railway, knew that if you could urge the fire to burn harder, you could extract every bit of heat out of it, and make the most of the potential performance of the locomotive. The secret lay with the blastpipe and chimney, part of the 'front end'. The blastpipe was the outlet for the steam exhausted from the cylinders, and as this steam went up and out of the chimney it dragged hot gases from the fire with it. The theory was simple: the faster you could get these exhaust gases moving, the more air they would draw through the boiler and firegrate, and the hotter the fire would burn. There would, in engineering terms, be less back-pressure on the hot gases leaving the firebox. There were a number of ways of achieving this, and all worked on the principle of splitting the flow of this exhaust gas in order to increase its surface area so it could draw more air with it. What Townend wanted to do was hardly original. One of the decisive contributory factors to *Mallard's* record-breaking run in 1938 had been its special exhaust arrangement – known as 'Kylchap', after its designers (Kylälä, from Finland, and the French locomotive genius, André Chapelon), which was a popular way of increasing power.

Initially – and unsurprisingly, as BR was a state-owned company – his request to fit 'Kylchap' exhausts to his fleet was refused on grounds of cost, but Townend persisted. He knew that by fitting them to the 'A3' and 'A4' 4-6-2s and as many others as possible, not only would performance improve, but coal consumption would fall too. In 1959 *Flying Scotsman* was fitted with a 'Kylchap' exhaust and the double chimney needed to accommodate it. The cost was just £153 per locomotive, and with coal savings of 6–7 lbs per mile, the railways very quickly made a profit on their expenditure.

It's ironic that in the twilight of their lives, performance of the 'A3s' had finally reached its potential. To all intents and purposes, on all but the most demanding of duties, they were every bit the equal of the 'A4s'. So much so that they returned to use on the prestigious titled trains to Newcastle and back, working duties of up to 546 miles a day with a turnaround time at Newcastle of just 55 minutes. By the standards of the day, this was a railway operating with the precision of a Swiss watch.

Townend, Top Shed and his 'Pacifics' should have been given the next decade to prove their worth, but, as dieselisation gathered pace, the days of Top Shed and its 'Pacifics' were numbered. Nobody knew quite when the axe would fall, but it was now a question of 'when' rather than 'if'. Time was running out.

The first British diesel locomotives were used for shunting, initially with the London, Midland and Scottish Railway (LMS) before the Second World War. In fact it was the LMS, the London and North Eastern Railway's great rival, that pioneered the use of powerful diesel locomotives for main line passenger services with a pair of locomotives built at Derby Works in 1947. These paved the way for future locomotives, but one in particular would cause the death of steam on the East Coast Main Line race track. Called Deltic, she was the most powerful diesel locomotive in the world at the time and she was also light and fast. Extensive trials showed that diesel traction could make a major difference to the speed and performance of trains, although Deltic herself was felt to be

Opposite Amongst the first main line diesels were the English Electric Type 4s. With around 2,000 horsepower, they were nominally more powerful than the steam 'Pacifics', but power losses incurred by generators and traction motors meant that in real terms they were little improvement on the old technology. Something more powerful was needed for the East Coast Main Line.

too expensive to build, and too time-consuming to maintain. When her engine failed, she was withdrawn from service.

Though BR was still building steam locomotives, in 1958 the first products of the ill-conceived Modernisation Plan were tentatively entering traffic, and unsurprisingly the East Coast Main Line was first in line to receive them. Known as English Electric Type 4s, these had a 2,000-horsepower engine and should have been able to put Gresley's steam locomotives in the shade, because on an average day an 'A3' like *Flying Scotsman* (now at her final shed at King's Cross) was able to put out around 1,500 horsepower. But it wasn't quite as simple as that. While all the power *Flying Scotsman* was able to generate went from the boiler to the pistons to the wheels, that 2,000 horsepower output of the diesels was absorbed, bit by bit, by onboard electrics and the generator used to power the electric motors that drove the wheels. So much so that, when it came to the power that reached the rail, these new diesels were only able to lay down 1,550 horsepower – no more, in practical terms, than the locomotives they were designed to replace.

With the Type 4s unable to reach the potential required for the East Coast Main Line services, BR turned back to the 'Deltic' concept. Between 1961 and 1962 the fleet of twenty-two locomotives carrying numbers D9000–D9022 entered traffic, slowly relegating steam to lesser duties and restricting it to certain areas. These 3,300-horsepower, 100-mph diesels had impressive characteristics for the early 1960s and rapidly revolutionised railway services on the East Coast Main Line both for the passengers and the crews. With the increase in speeds, infrastructure was also upgraded to reduce journey times between major cities.

The cab of a diesel was a world away from the dirty, hot and uncomfortable confines of a steam locomotive footplate. Now the driver needed to have a heater in the cab for colder months, but he also got much better vision, a comfortable chair, windscreen wipers and, most importantly, a clean atmosphere in which to work. The controls were much simpler to follow, and in some ways (although driving a train is never easy) much easier to operate. Now, rather than having to coax the best out of a locomotive, the diesel power units and electric traction motors

BRITISH RAILWAYS' AMBITIOUS GAMBLE

In 1955 BR embarked on a bold Modernisation Plan. The idea was that the higher purchase costs of diesel and electric trains would be outweighed by their higher availability for traffic, lower operating costs and potential for higher sustained speeds. Widespread electrification would take place on key routes and elsewhere steam locomotives would be replaced by diesel locomotives and multiple units (self-propelled carriages with cabs at each end of the train). Initial plans were for gradual implementation but pressure to get the system up and running meant that orders for new designs were often placed before they could be properly tested. The results were mixed. Some designs proved reliable and successful, but others suffered huge reliability problems. Many of the types ordered offered little if any performance advantages over steam. This, together with the unreliability of some fleets, led to the withdrawal and scrapping of diesel locomotives before BR eliminated its steam fleet.

did the physical work for the driver, and power could be increased virtually at the touch of a button, rather than through preparation of the fire and boiler pressure.

It was a new and bold era, where diesel designs were tried and tested in service to evaluate performance. The irony was that the Modernisation Plan effectively wasted money just as much as the final years of the steam locomotive construction programme, because yet more money was spent on diesel designs that didn't reach the desired potential, leading to their early withdrawal. Some designs fared much better and became the staple of the BR motive power fleet, and even today there are locomotives that originated in the early 1960s continuing in service on the main line, admirably doing the job they were built for. With the dawn of the Modernisation Plan, however, the future was bleak for steam, and *Flying Scotsman*.

Left The solution was found in the 3,300-horsepower 'Deltic' diesels. Based on a 1950s prototype these were the machines that finally eliminated steam haulage on the flagship expresses from King's Cross. In summer 1964, No. D9020 *Nimbus* carries the golden fibreglass headboard which proclaims it is working 'The Flying Scotsman'. It is departing York.

Above The cab of prototype diesel 'Deltic', built in 1955. Production versions of this were delivered in 1961–62 and were a world away from the heat, draught and dirt of a steam locomotive cab. The view forward over the tall bonnet was less than ideal, however.

7

KNIGHT IN SHINING ARMOUR

I n 1924 the wealthy owners of the Northern Rubber company in Retford took their four-year-old son to the Wembley exhibition. Though he must have been dazzled by the exhibits, one stood out above all others: the apple green *Flying Scotsman*.

'I gazed up at this huge gleaming machine and was lifted into its cab. I remember being impressed at how clean it was compared with the grimier engines we saw at home, and how marvellous its apple-green paint was compared

with the smaller engine alongside it [*Caerphilly Castle*]. I was spellbound, and couldn't stop thinking about it all the way home,' he recalled in an interview in *The Railway Magazine*.

As he grew up, Alan Pegler got to know the staff at his nearest station, Barnby Moor, and became a keen and extremely proficient photographer. Thanks to his family's wealth got a private pilot' s licence when he was just seventeen. To nobody's surprise, the young Pegler

Below The saviour of *Flying Scotsman*, Alan Pegler, applies Brasso to the locomotive's nameplate on 18 April 1964 at London Marylebone. Pegler was the first private individual to buy such a large locomotive from British Railways (BR).

used it to chase trains from the air: always, of course, his beloved LNER (London and North Eastern Railway). The impact made by *Flying Scotsman* in the 1920s still loomed large over this young man.

Wartime brought a posting to the Fleet Air Arm, and, thanks to his private pilot's licence, Pegler became a pilot flying Skua dive-bombers. Appendicitis curtailed his flying career, but he transferred to the Royal Observer Corps, which he was involved in throughout the 1950s and 1960s. In late 1946, he was demobilised and went back to Retford and Northern Rubber. The company had no links with railways, but Pegler's office window overlooked the Sheffield to Lincoln railway; his passion for railways, dormant since the war, started to return. His duties at Northern Rubber were far from taxing, as the company largely ran itself, and he had a good income and time on his hands, but it wasn't until he travelled on a special train run by British Railways (BR) to mark the centenary of the main line of the Great Northern Railway (GNR) in 1950 that his enthusiasm for the railway really reignited.

In 1950 it was Northern Rubber's eightieth anniversary, and Pegler decided he would plan an excursion for the company's staff. This wasn't a particularly unusual thing to do back then: plenty of big companies organised day trips for their staff. The first of Pegler's specials ran from Retford to London in May 1951 to take staff to the Festival of Britain. Further excursions saw him taking former LNER locomotives to destinations as far away as Blackpool: the staff must have loved him. Pegler had by now well and truly got the railway bug back.

At this point, Pegler was little more than a generous employer taking his staff on trips. But in September 1952 he did something really unusual. With a friend, Trevor Bailey, he arranged with the Eastern Region of BR to run a special train to celebrate the centenary of the line between Retford, Newark and Grantham. On 28 September a train hauled by 'A4' 60007 *Sir Nigel Gresley* took 400 railway enthusiasts to the old railway museum (the current National Railway Museum opened only in the 1970s) in York. It was a rare thing back then – a special, chartered train where bookings were open to the public. It was a complete contrast with the private specials run by companies, and it heralded the proper start of today's charter train business.

Pegler had a ready market for these trips. He was president of the Gainsborough Model Railway Society, one of the pre-eminent organisations of its type in the country at the time. Alan Burton joined the society in 1949 aged eleven: 'It was quite exciting – I'd just been given my very first model. I didn't know anybody to start with, but everybody was of a like mind, and I was one of the young "erks." We were told Alan Pegler had been named President, and this big rosy-faced chap walked in – he was one of those people who lights up a room the moment he walks in.'

Opposite The Talyllyn Railway was the first to be preserved and run by volunteers. This view in 1955 – the year of BR's Modernisation Plan – shows the rustic engine shed at Towyn Pendre.

A year later, Pegler really surpassed himself by persuading the powers that be on the Eastern Region to remove two historic locomotives from the York Museum – two old GNR 'Atlantics' – restore them to working order, and use them to double-head a train from King's Cross to Doncaster to celebrate the centenary of the famous Doncaster Works where *Flying Scotsman* was built.

Five hundred enthusiasts crammed the first train, and it was so popular that a second train ran from Leeds to London a week later. The stage was set for Pegler to run more charters, and with official blessing too. Specials began to run all over the country, taking people like Alan Burton to parts of the country they would never otherwise have seen. Pegler loved it, and seemingly enjoyed having the money to do it: 'It was something different,' says Burton, 'it was like a big toy for him, and I never saw him unhappy on the trains.'

One of the passengers on Pegler's charters was a buffet-car steward who regularly served the deputy chairman of the British Transport Commission (BTC), Sir John Benstead, on a morning train from Grantham to King's Cross. The steward's enthusiasm for these special trains must have proved contagious, because Benstead recommended Pegler to BTC Chairman Sir Brian Robertson for a place on a newly established regional board. BR, it seemed, was delighted that Pegler was giving the Eastern Region such a positive public image, so Sir Brian agreed, and, even though Pegler was seventeen years younger than any other member, he was offered a place as a part-time member of the Eastern Region Area Board. 'It was astonishing really … complete luck!' enthused Pegler, who had finally succeeded in making a career out of the railway.

Before his appointment, however, Pegler had already been busy on an altogether different kind of railway in distant Wales. Around the world, railways with narrower tracks have long been popular, as they allow tighter curves

to be built, and require less substantial engineering to construct and maintain. In Britain, because standard-gauge railways were already so well-established, narrow-gauge lines only really gained a foothold in the mountainous area of North Wales, where the need to transport huge quantities of slate from the mountain quarries to ports had seen a number of them established.

By the early 1950s, just a couple were in operation: one, from Aberystwyth to Devil's Bridge, was owned by BR. The other, from Tywyn to Abergynolwyn, was owned privately, and was on its last legs. A daring attempt to operate the latter (known as the Talyllyn Railway) as a volunteer-run tourist attraction had started in 1951, and a chance conversation between one of its pioneers, Lord Northesk, and Pegler on the July centenary train in 1950 saw Pegler gravitate inexorably to the Ffestiniog Railway, which ran from Porthmadog to Blaenau Ffestiniog. This, asserted Northesk, was the line the Talyllyn volunteers had wanted to restore. For Pegler, the challenge was irresistible.

This 13.5-mile line had been built in the nineteenth century to transport slate (and later passengers), and it's said that this picturesque, sinuous and hilly route helped roof the empire. It had a gauge of a fraction under 2 feet (compared with the standard gauge of 4 feet 8½ inches) but was far from a toy railway. The war had taken its toll, though, and with little of the tourist traffic on which it had come to depend, and with quarries turning to lorries, the line had closed in August 1946, with track, engines and carriages abandoned where they lay. Pegler visited it in 1952, and nothing had changed.

Legal issues and debts made reopening the Ffestiniog extremely difficult but, thanks to an interest-free loan from his father, Alan Pegler was able to acquire and resurrect it. Suddenly, Pegler's dream of reopening the old, almost forgotten Ffestiniog was alive and kicking. In June 1954 he gained his controlling interest, which he subsequently transferred to a charitable trust. It was the first railway line in Britain to have closed and then been reopened by railway enthusiasts (the pioneering Talyllyn was kept open, thanks to the early efforts of dedicated supporters). The Ffestiniog set the pattern for much of the preservation movement that was to follow, and it is thanks to Pegler's generosity, ingenuity, and outright passion that it reopened when it did. Not for nothing is Pegler regarded by many as the founding father of railway preservation.

Pegler took up his appointment on the Eastern Region Area Board in 1955, the year of the much-vaunted Modernisation Plan. It was an auspicious moment: railway enthusiasts were often greeted with suspicion by senior management, but in Pegler, they had inadvertently appointed *Flying Scotsman's* greatest fan. Without his appointment to the area board, it now seems unlikely that *Flying Scotsman* would have survived.

Below Alan Pegler acquired an interest-free loan from his father to resurrect the Ffestiniog Railway in 1951 – the first time a closed railway had been reinstated by volunteers. In 1925 it was still operating as a going concern but declining traffic would see it close after the Second World War. This is the scene at Portmadoc New, with Ffestiniog trains passing in 1925.

The distractions of the board, and of the Ffestiniog, which he would hold the chairmanship of until 1972, were diverting Alan Pegler too much from his day job at Northern Rubber however. After his father died in 1957 the other members of the family became increasingly concerned that Pegler Junior wasn't spending enough time on the business. Peglers of Doncaster, a firm operated by another part of the family, finally took over Northern Rubber in 1961. Alan Pegler's share of the deal was £70,000 – the equivalent to £500,000 or so today.

By the early 1960s, steam was starting to leave the stage. The planned phased replacement of steam under the Modernisation Plan was becoming outright slaughter. Already, thousands of serviceable, economic locomotives had been sacrificed, and as the new diesels entered service the scrapman's hunger became a feeding frenzy. In 1947, the year before nationalisation, there had been around 20,000 steam locomotives in service on Britain's main line railways (a figure that doesn't include the many thousands of locomotives used by industry). A decade later, there were still almost 17,000, although diesels were starting to make an impact in places, but that remaining 17,000 would all be gone by August 1968. It was extinction on a cataclysmic scale.

The Western Region was first to really make inroads into its steam fleet but by the early 1960s the Eastern Region of BR (formerly the LNER) was also feeling the pinch, and with the introduction of the high-speed 100mph production 'Deltic' diesels in 1961, time was called on express steam designs, including the streamlined 'A4s' and their 'A3' counterparts. The 'A3s' were relegated to lesser duties or withdrawn, whilst the 'A4s' received a stay of execution, hauling express trains between Edinburgh and Aberdeen. On the East Coast Main Line, though, steam was all but gone.

As diesels were introduced steam was gradually run down not just in numbers, but also in maintenance. By 1960 steam locomotives were becoming sufficiently outmoded that maintenance was reduced; in some cases the mechanical condition was allowed to deteriorate, and external appearances left a lot to be desired. They still had a job to do, but their appearance certainly reflected the incoming tide of new diesels. The golden age of steam was truly over, and it was only a matter of time until steam was completely eradicated from main line work. The first of *Flying Scotsman's* sister engines, No. 60104 *Solario*, succumbed as early as 1959.

Historically, when locomotives were withdrawn from service, they were scrapped by the railway itself at one of its locomotive works. Any parts that couldn't be reused were melted down and turned into new locomotives. Now, though, the railway works – already at capacity, thanks to the diesel building programme – simply couldn't cope with this mass extinction. Queues of forlorn steam locomotives lined the sidings of places like Swindon, Doncaster, Crewe and Darlington, often with their connecting rods cut and their fires dead, awaiting their inevitable fate.

When the end came for a steam locomotive, it was never pretty. Not for these gallant machines the dignity of being disassembled into their component parts. It was brutal. Standing wherever they could, the scrapmen torched holes in the metalwork that had been so diligently formed, joined, maintained and operated over the years. Boiler tubes were severed like veins, the valve gear amputated, and the wheels gas-axed, all in the name of progress.

As withdrawals accelerated, private scrap merchants were encouraged to buy these old steam locomotives from BR and scrap them themselves. Macabre cavalcades of dead steam locomotives moved to these scrapyards, often hauled by a locomotive also doomed to have its fire dropped in the scrapyard for the last time and then join the others in the scrap lines.

In recognition of the rapid fall of steam, the BTC decided to save a number of locomotives, carriages and wagons for posterity in order to tell the story of Britain's railways to future generations. It had to strike a balance between telling the story of Britain's railways, saving historically significant designs, and ensuring that there would be some-where to keep what it had saved. Bear in mind that the only preserved railways at this time were the narrow-gauge

Talyllyn and Ffestiniog Railways (totally unusable for storage of standard-gauge equipment); the standard-gauge Middleton Railway near Leeds, and the extremely embryonic Bluebell Railway near Horsted Keynes.

Inevitably, there were tough decisions. The London, Midlands and Scottish Railway lost its 'Patriots', 'Royal Scots', and 'Princesses', the Great Western Railway (GWR) missed out on its 'Halls', 'Manors', 'Granges' and 'Moguls'. BR was well-represented, as was the Southern Railway (SR), but for the LNER, there were some huge gaps. A place in posterity was assured for the record-breaker, No. 4468 *Mallard*, and for the pioneering 'V2', *Green Arrow*, but there was no room for the ultimate expression of LNER

locomotive design – the Peppercorn-designed 'A1' – nor for Gresley's freight designs, nor one of Thompson's go-anywhere 'B1s'. But the most glaring omission, the most inexcusable, was that none of Gresley's first Pacifics' – the first, and arguably the most successful 'Pacifics' in Britain – was on the list for preservation. It was a scandal. The reason given at the time was that only one locomotive of a given wheel-arrangement per designer could be preserved – patent nonsense, given that both *Caerphilly Castle* and *King George V* of the GWR (both 4-6-0s) had been listed for preservation, as well as two SR 4-6-0s.

The BTC, it seems, looked at preserving *Great Northern* but, because of Thompson's alterations, rejected her on the grounds of suitability and cost of conversion. They may also have felt that, as an 'A3' wasn't the original design Gresley had penned in 1922, the type was unsuitable anyway. Nonetheless, two 'A3s' could each have justified a place on the list: the 108-mph *Papyrus* and, more important still, the record-breaking *Flying Scotsman*, the most viewed, and probably the most loved of all. They were denied it because the BTC felt that Gresley's big designs were suitably represented by *Mallard* and *Green Arrow*.

Enthusiasts around the country were outraged and sought to persuade the BTC to change its mind. There was a precedent for this when the flamboyant secretary of the Gainsborough Model Railway Society, George Hinchcliffe, led a massive letter-writing campaign that persuaded the BTC to save one of the old Great Central's delightful 'Director' class (so called because they were named after directors of the company), *Butler-Henderson*. Pegler, thanks to his place on the Eastern Region Area Board, had also lobbied hard to preserve *Butler-Henderson* in the 1950s, and had ultimately been successful. Since then, Pegler had been keeping a watchful eye on the BTC's list, and had asked the Eastern Region's general manager to let him

left A modern day scene on the Ffestiniog Railway. It links to the Welsh Highland Railway and together constitutes the longest heritage railway in Britain.

know if anything was heard about *Flying Scotsman's* future.

When the list was published in 1961, Pegler, like many others, was aghast: 'The situation was intolerable. I was horrified at the prospect of seeing this marvellous class wiped out, and I resolved that if the State wouldn't correct this injustice, then I jolly well would!' Others felt the same, and in Scotland a group of railway enthusiasts led by Ramsey Ferguson decided to form a society to preserve an 'A3'. They started raising money, and, thanks to publicity in railway magazines of the time, donations started to come in. In October 1962 they revealed that they wanted to preserve *Flying Scotsman* and started the first 'Save Our Scotsman' appeal; within eight weeks more than 300 people had joined, and almost £1,000 had been raised – not bad at a time when £10 a week was considered a good wage. The group was nothing if not ambitious, for it was an astonishing notion that a private group of individuals could buy something as massive and complicated as a steam locomotive. It must have been hard at times to prove they were serious – but they needed to, because time was running out.

Just weeks later BR announced that the pioneer 'A4' 4-6-2, *Silver Link*, was destined for the cutter's torch, and then, in December, Pegler received a letter from the Eastern Region. It was bad news. *Flying Scotsman* was going to be withdrawn for scrap in January. She was available for purchase before then, but she would cost the whopping sum of £3,000, and the 'A3' society had only raised £1,000. Pegler felt he had to act, and within forty-eight hours of receiving the letter, he hot-footed it to Scotland to meet Ferguson. He asked straight: 'Can you raise the extra £2,000?' Ferguson was equally honest in return. 'No,' he said. For a second, time stood still as Pegler weighed, for the last time, the decision he was about to make. Should he take the plunge and spend a huge amount on a steam locomotive he didn't need, had nowhere to keep, and little chance of running – or should he keep his wallet closed and trust to providence that some-body else would save this icon?

He'd probably made his mind up soon after receiving the letter from the Eastern Region, but his heart must have been beating a tattoo as he told Ferguson, as calmly as he could, that he was going to try to buy *Flying Scotsman* – and, not only that, was going to attempt to keep her running on the main line. For his part, Ferguson must have had mixed feelings: delight that the locomotive might be saved, and sadness that his group's bold and daring bid to secure her was now out of the running. Ferguson would later be instrumental in setting up the Gresley Society and preserving some of the engineer's lesser-known designs.

So *Flying Scotsman* had side-stepped the scrapman at the very last minute. Pegler returned from Scotland and swiftly sealed the sale. There were to be no discounts on the £3,000 asking price, even to an area board member,

but he resolved to get some extras thrown in as part of the purchase price.

With express passenger steam on the old LNER main line rapidly fading away with the entry into traffic of the 3,300-horsepower 'Deltic' diesels, there must have been mixed feelings in the corridors of power of the Eastern Region about this swift and brutal transfer. Progress was one thing, but traditions built up over decades were being swept away. Somebody must have felt inclined to make a gesture in favour of steam, because the sale of *Flying Scotsman* was handled directly by the Eastern Region and not by BR's Central Supplies department, which handled

Above As steam locomotives were withdrawn en masse, convoys of locomotives were taken for scrap. Often the leading locomotive would have its fire dropped at the scrapyard and then succumb to the cutter's torch itself. On 14 September 1964 'V2' No. 60941 passes Ruddington on the Great Central Main Line with three classmates en route to Swindon for scrapping.

all sales after that. In return for his £3,000, Pegler got *Flying Scotsman* herself, and, just as crucially, she was given a complete overhaul, converted back to single-chimney form and repainted into the colour that suited her best: LNER apple-green. He even got two main line test runs from Doncaster to Peterborough and back thrown in. Added together, the extras can't have been worth much less than the locomotive: it was a great deal.

Ferguson had kept the Save Our Scotsman fund running in case Pegler wasn't successful, or changed his mind, and efforts were still being made to raise money. Pegler was president of the Gainsborough Model Railway Society, one of the most respected institutions of its type in the country then, and it was at its annual dinner that the first mention of the impending purchase was made. Pegler was passed a plate for donations to the Save Our Scotsman campaign but, to the shock of the members, he politely declined to contribute. Surely, they must have wondered, their president (and a very wealthy man to boot) couldn't possibly refuse to support such a worthy cause, could he?

Pegler, conscious of the reaction, leaned over to the Society's secretary, George Hinchcliffe, and whispered *sotto voce*: 'Sorry about that, but the reason I didn't donate was that I've just bought the whole blooming engine!' After a few seconds absorbing the shock, Hinchcliffe recovered and the dinner continued unabated.

Above right Before the end of the 1950s Pegler and volunteers at the Ffestiniog Railway had transformed dereliction into a stunning tourist attraction that continues to enthral to the present day.

Right The record-breaking 'A4' No. 60022 *Mallard* waits for departure from London King's Cross on 2 June 1962 with the Railway Correspondence and Travel Society/Stephenson Locomotive Society 'Aberdeen Flier' rail tour. This locomotive was saved for the nation and restored to 1930s condition.

Below One of Gresley's best designs was the 'V2' 2-6-2. Designed for general duties, these superb locomotives were almost the equal of the 'A3' 4-6-2s despite being smaller. The pioneer, No. 4771 *Green Arrow* was saved for the nation – sufficient justification for the British Transport Commission not to save an 'A3'. It is now out of service, but in the 1980s the locomotive was used on regular charter duties on the main line. *Green Arrow* is shown here hauling a York to Scarborough special train during this period.

Opposite A leaflet for the Save our Scotsman campaign. It was unable to raise sufficient funds to buy the locomotive – and No. 60103's future looked bleak until Pegler stepped in.

SAVE OUR SCOTSMAN

The Gresley A3 Pacific " Flying Scotsman " is due for the scrapheap

RAILWAY ENTHUSIASTS THIS MUST NOT BE

★ **Lovely to Look at**

The first engine to be painted in L.N.E.R. green, she emerged from the Doncaster shops in January, 1923, the forerunner of this class of five engines. Another distinction was that she was the only engine to have bright polished wheel centres and tyres (rims) and polished brass splasher beadings. She even became a film star at Watton, Herts, in the spring of 1928.

★ **History is Made**

On May Day, 1928, at 10 a.m., she pulled out of King's Cross at the head of her namesake train, and by early evening had completed the first-ever world record non-stop run of 393 miles to Waverley. Previously a new type high-sided corridor tender had been fitted with a capacity of 9 tons of coal and 5000 gallons of water. In running trim she then turned the scales at just under 159 tons.

★ **Her Finest Hour**

Coaxed by Driver Bill Sparshatt and Fireman Webster of King's Cross sheds, she created a record run on November 30, 1934, on a test trip from King's Cross to Leeds and back. Allowed 165 minutes for the $185\frac{1}{2}$ miles, 4472 bettered this timing by $13\frac{1}{2}$ minutes. Given her head on the descent from Stoke Summit on the return trip, speed was maintained at 100 m.p.h. for some distance between Little Bytham and Essendine.

★ **Everybody's Darling**

To quote H. C. Casserley, " 4472 was one of the best known of the whole lot, and already became ' Flying Scotsman ' after the train of that name, which it frequently worked." Driven by electric motors, 4472 ran continuously at the 1924 Wembley Exhibition, where she was the star L.N.E.R. exhibit.

THERE THEN ARE THE FACTS

£3000

WOULD SAVE THE " SCOTSMAN " FOR PERMANENT DISPLAY

YOU CAN HELP NOW

Send your donation to—

DOUGLAS J. SPENCE (Treasurer),
52 Stirling Road, Edinburgh, 5.
GRESLEY " A3 " PRESERVATION SOCIETY

Printed by Herald Press, Arbroath.

8

INDIAN SUMMER

Though Pegler understandably wanted to keep it quiet, the deal was too good to stay a secret for long, and within weeks this rich businessman from Retford became national news: the first person to buy such a big locomotive in Britain. And he was only just in time, because *Flying Scotsman*'s last revenue-earning train for British Railways (BR) was to be the 13:15 King's Cross to Leeds on 14 January 1963.

The public's imagination had been fired by this former pilot indulging his passion for steam. There were journalists, newsreel cameras and photographers everywhere, even film cameras from as far away as the United States and Canada: King's Cross had seldom been so busy.

Pegler, inevitably, was at the centre of things. He spent two bitterly freezing hours at Top Shed, where, in footplate crew overalls, he did interview after interview. Eventually the moment came for *Flying Scotsman* to leave Top Shed for the last time in public ownership and reverse on to her train. Everywhere that there was a vantage point, crowds amassed to say *au revoir*. The Station Master had his top hat on, people thronged the tracks: it was like a royal occasion. Perhaps, in a sense, it was.

As departure time approached, Pegler stood on the footplate with a red carnation in his hand and signed autographs. 'It was the proudest day of my life,' he said. On the stroke of a quarter past one the guard blew his whistle, and, with a hiss of steam from the cylinder draincocks and just the faintest hint of a slip, *Flying Scotsman* took her final public train north.

From the footbridges of Finsbury Park to the platforms of Potters Bar and the streets of Stevenage, thousands of well-wishers braved the cold to mark the grand finale of East Coast Main Line steam. (It wasn't the last steam-hauled train from King's Cross, true, but it was the last hurrah, and the public wanted to mark it.)

A newsreel crew accompanied the train, and their film shows that the crowds really had to be seen to be believed. At Peterborough, their cheers can clearly be heard on the soundtrack, and the station was absolutely packed. After the stop at Peterborough *Flying Scotsman* dug her heels in and gritted her teeth in preparation for the climb up Stoke Bank – the same hill where *Mallard* had beaten the Germans so many years before – and then on towards Retford, which she passed 4 minutes early.

Then, at the level crossing at the now-closed Barnby Moor and Sutton station, the site of Pegler's earliest railway

Below *Flying Scotsman* passes under the A19 at Selby in 1968, the year that British Railways (BR) eliminated main line steam. From 11 August that year No. 4472 would be the only steam locomotive allowed on BR metals outside London, where London Transport retained some for engineering duties.

Following pages After overhaul at Doncaster Works, No. 4472 – now repainted in the old London and North Eastern Railway apple green – stretches her legs for the first time in preservation at Harringay station on 19 April 1963. She would work her first rail tour on the following day.

memories, Pegler hung on the whistle chain for what seemed like minutes in noisy acknowledgement of his family and friends, who had gathered for a rather chilly and unseasonal picnic. It was proving to be an epic run, but it had to come to an end, and as she slowed for the approaches to Doncaster the enormity of what he had done must have hit Pegler: he had saved an icon that had irrefutably demonstrated how loved it really was. She arrived at Doncaster 6 minutes early, and was uncoupled from the train to be replaced by another locomotive. She then went more or less straight into the works where she was built for overhaul.

Doncaster Works showed just what they could do, giving *Flying Scotsman* a complete overhaul in just twenty-four days, and at the end of February 1963, now restored to her original single-chimney form, she undertook two trial runs from Doncaster to Peterborough and back. She hadn't yet been repainted, and she looked somewhat forlorn, but mechanically speaking she was now in mint condition and raring to go. Pegler, who was on the footplate on both runs, looked the part of her proud owner, brimming with confidence and pride.

She finally emerged from Doncaster works, like a butterfly from a chrysalis, on 26 March 1963, and it was clear her links with BR were severed. The dull Brunswick green paint had been replaced by sparkling apple green, and she had acquired a corridor tender from one of the remaining streamlined 'A4s'. She was absolutely immaculate, and Pegler must have felt, for a moment at least, that it would be a crying shame to run her and spoil the craftsman's finish on her!

Pegler's plan was to run *Flying Scotsman* on charter trains across the network, but to do that he needed to get a deal with BR. His solicitor drew up heads of agreement with the chief solicitor of the BR Board, and while it didn't immediately allow Pegler to do anything at all, it did provide the contractual process to make it happen. One of its provisos was that Pegler could run *Flying Scotsman* on BR until 1966, with options that could take it up to 1971. This was crucial for Pegler, because at the time, there was simply nowhere else he could run her! He had also agreed to lease a former locomotive weigh-house at the end of Platform 8 at Doncaster for £65 per year. All this was handled by the Deputy Chairman of the BR Board, Sir Stuart Mitchell. Mitchell was supportive of *Flying Scotsman* – 'he

left No. 4472 comes off shed at Staveley Barrow Hill before working 'The Palatine' back to St Pancras on 18 November 1967.

thought it would be rather fun,' recalls Pegler – and put the plans in motion, neglecting, whether by accident or design, to tell his boss. His boss, the chairman of the BR Board, was a balding man with a toothbrush moustache called Dr Beeching.

Beeching is most famous for recommending the closure of 6,000 miles of Britain's 18,000-mile rail network in a bid to solve BR's rising annual deficit. The cuts weren't always rational – had the Great Central Main Line remained open the proposed High Speed 2 railway might not be needed – or fair, with huge areas of the country stripped of their

railways forever. Beeching didn't undertake the cuts though: that was down to politicians seeking a short-term fix without the slightest regard for what might be needed in the future. For the railways it has always been thus.

Ironically, though, the carnage wreaked on the rail network in the 1960s ultimately benefited *Flying Scotsman*, because it paved the way for the railway preservation movement to flourish. Without those closed routes abandoned for preservationists in the 1960s and 1970s to reopen, and the lines of steam locomotives abandoned at Barry Scrapyard, Wales, there would have been many fewer

Below On her last day in British Railways (BR) service, 14 January 1963, 'A3' 4-6-2 No. 60103 *Flying Scotsman* prepares to haul her train from London King's Cross as far as Doncaster, where she would be overhauled for new owner Alan Pegler.

Right Richard Beeching's plan to close a third of the rail network drew stinging protests, such as this in Manchester on 13 October 1963. They were to no avail and the axe was wielded, leaving huge areas of the country without any railways at all.

places to see steam in action, and many fewer locomotives to see in the first place.

Perhaps Pegler's most outstanding achievement, however, was not buying *Flying Scotsman*, or even the extras on the deal: it was the extraordinary deal he struck with BR to run *Flying Scotsman* on the main line. Beeching was furious at this. He found out about Mitchell's agreement with Pegler for the weigh-house at Doncaster and, in Pegler's words, hit the roof: 'He'd obviously not read the newspapers properly in January!' Beeching saw Pegler as a dangerous maverick who could tarnish the image of BR and must be stopped. The railways were in the midst of a painful process of modernisation, and in the early 1960s – when all the talk was of the space race, the Cold War, the white heat of technology – the steam railway looked very, very old. Running *Flying Scotsman* on the network, Beeching argued, would send out entirely the wrong message about Britain's railways, and should not be allowed, so he immediately forbade Pegler to run *Flying Scotsman* on the main line. Pegler countered with the contract signed with the BR Board's chief solicitor, and Beeching, outwitted, issued a stern directive banning future deals similar to *Flying Scotsman's* from being signed.

It seems that Beeching was also upset that it was an area board member who had signed this deal. He decided to fire Pegler because running a steam locomotive was detrimental to the railway: the exact reverse of Sir Brian Robertson's reason for appointing him. Pegler asked for a head-to-head meeting with Beeching.

'I'd just like to know for my own satisfaction,' Pegler asked him, 'is the reason I'm being dropped from the area board anything to do with the fact that I bought *Flying Scotsman*?'

Beeching sat back in his chair and looked Pegler straight in the eye. After a pause that must have felt, even to Pegler, like a thousand years, he responded:

'Well, as a matter of fact, yes.'

'Thanks very much,' said Pegler. 'That's all I wanted to know.'

Pegler, still an extremely wealthy man, wasn't fazed by this official disapproval, and swiftly moved to ensure that *Flying Scotsman* got the tender loving care she deserved. To look after her, he hired the retired Doncaster driver Edgar Hoyle, who on an epic run with 'A4' No. 4498 *Sir Nigel Gresley* in the 1950s was running well at 112mph and looking in good form to beat *Mallard* when the locomotive inspector eased the regulator. To help run the tours he had in mind for *Flying Scotsman* he also brought in George Hinchcliffe, a school teacher, who in his spare time was Secretary of the Gainsborough Model Railway Society. Hinchcliffe had worked with Pegler for years, first helping to market rail tours in the 1950s, and from 1963 promoting

Flying Scotsman too. He was an enthusiast almost from birth, and as he grew up he proved an expert blagger of footplate rides and a naturally brilliant fireman. War service interrupted his engineering apprenticeship, and when he returned from the Navy he became a teacher instead. Without Hinchcliffe, Pegler and *Flying Scotsman* would not have been nearly as successful, and Pegler's decision to appoint him was nothing short of inspired.

Everything was now in place, and in honour of the Ffestiniog Railway, Pegler planned the first train in private ownership to take enthusiasts from London Paddington to Wales to see Pegler's spectacular narrow-gauge line.

On the morning of 20 April 1963, *Flying Scotsman* backed on to her train in Brunel's cathedral to steam at Paddington. She was probably the first ex-London and North Eastern Railway (LNER) 'Pacific' locomotive to visit the station since No. 60033 *Seagull* in the 1948 locomotive exchanges, and she was almost certainly the first of Gresley's initial design of 'Pacific' to visit since 'A1' No. 4474 *Victor Wild* back in 1925. To the local enthusiasts, by then more used to diesels than steam, *Flying Scotsman* was a poignant reminder of past glories, and they came in their droves to witness this unusual and stirring sight.

As she headed north, it was clear that the public's enthusiasm for the old lady had, if anything, grown since her last run in BR service. Though undoubtedly helped by the fact that an 'A3' was a complete stranger to these lines, crowds flocked to every vantage point they could to see her. At Birmingham's much-missed old Snow Hill station, 8,000 fans (a football crowd, according to one commentator) jammed the platforms, footbridges and even the tracks to get a glimpse – and Snow Hill was a pretty big station then. Such were the numbers that the police had to be called in to keep order. And so it went on, up through Shrewsbury, on the main line of the old Great Western Railway (GWR) to Chester, as far as Ruabon, where *Flying Scotsman* had to give way to a smaller locomotive because of weight and size restrictions on the line through mid-Wales. It was the first time this queen of locomotives had visited the Principality. If Pegler had had any doubts in his mind whatsoever about the appeal of *Flying Scotsman*, they were well and truly blown away by the end of the journey.

In May the second tour ran, this time for the Gainsborough Model Railway Society, which had supported Pegler so steadfastly. It ran from Lincoln to Southampton – more new territory for *Flying Scotsman* – and the scenes from the first run were repeated. Everyone wanted to get a glimpse of *Flying Scotsman*, it seemed. More and more tours ran, and Pegler was in his element, playing the part of showman to perfection. He would go through the train talking to passengers, signing books, and adored seeing smiling, happy children on them. Charities also benefited, particularly in one spectacular run a couple of years later.

AN ICON ON AN ICON

When Alan Pegler wanted a painting of *Flying Scotsman* he turned to one of the greatest railway artists ever, Terence Cuneo (1907–96). The location was to be the Forth Bridge in Scotland but it seemed unlikely that BR would allow the locomotive to occupy the bridge while Cuneo worked his magic on canvas. Pegler asked Scottish Region boss Willie Thorpe if he could 'borrow' the bridge for a couple of days and amazingly Thorpe agreed. 'And it caused absolute chaos!' said Pegler: 'It was sort of sat on the Forth Bridge for about three days and had to get out of the way of the fish train from Aberdeen, which in those days was still running, and various other things – but it was an extraordinary experience.' Cuneo painted another portrait of *Flying Scotsman* in the 1960s, this time of Alan Pegler at the throttle of the locomotive. Cuneo's statue stands at London Waterloo station.

The tours continued, and in 1964 *Flying Scotsman* visited her namesake country for the first time in twenty-five years. Pegler chartered the prestigious 'Master Cutler' carriages to run a special 'Pegler's Pullman' train from Doncaster to Edinburgh Waverley, a run well within the locomotive's capabilities. She wasn't the only steam locomotive on the old East Coast Main Line on 9 May 1964, but she was one of an ever-shrinking handful: the last few Gresley 'Pacifics' were going out in a last blaze of glory on the difficult and strenuous line from Edinburgh to Aberdeen.

By the end of 1964, *Flying Scotsman* had covered enough miles to need an intermediate overhaul, but her birthplace at Doncaster was no longer able to perform the necessary work. She would have to go north, to the old North Eastern Railway (NER) works at Darlington. Here, continuing the proud NER tradition, she had her cylinder casings painted green, something that had never been done before on a Gresley 'Pacific'. It was a sign of affection from the staff: the hatchet between the old Great Northern Railway and NER had finally been buried.

The start of 1965 really marked the beginning of the end of the steam railway. Most of the grand old classes – the GWR's 'Kings' and 'Castles', the 'Duchesses' and 'Princesses' of the London, Midland and Scottish Railway (LMS), the LNER 'Pacifics' – had gone or were well on their way out. Only the Southern Region, which had arguably the most modern express steam locomotives and wanted to keep them until electrification of key routes was complete, really supported steam. Most of the steam locomotives left were either heavy freight locomotives (invariably the LMS '8F' or BR '9F' types) or mixed-traffic locomotives along the lines of Thompson's 'B1'. This made *Flying Scotsman* more precious than ever, because now, with one or two exceptions, wherever she went she would be the only express steam passenger locomotive around. She was also a massive contrast with the increasingly filthy, ever more work-stained survivors of steam in BR service. Unlike them, she was immaculate.

Many years before, the GWR ran a Cheltenham to London express with the highest average speed of any train in the world at the time, around 71mph. The train was invariably hauled by a 'Castle', and the Western Region remained proud of its past glories. However, since the record had been set, Gresley's 'Pacifics' had been transformed by better boilers, valves and draughting. Pegler reckoned, with good reason, that on a similar five-coach train, *Flying Scotsman* ought to be able to smash the GWR's long-standing record, even within the 80mph speed limit imposed on the engine by BR.

A tour organised by *The Railway Magazine* on 9 October 1965 from Paddington to the Welsh Valleys provided the opportunity, and in anticipation of an epoch-making run, a TV crew hired a plane to film *Flying Scotsman*. The journey started well, with a clear run; the 36 miles to Reading was

done in just 32 minutes – not much slower than the 25-or-so minutes diesel trains take today – and it looked like the record attempt was most definitely on. *Flying Scotsman* was absolutely flying along the Great Western Main Line, motion blurring with the speed, and the chimney simmering with exhaust. As she approached Swindon, the atmosphere on the train started to bubble as the passengers started to realise just how well they were running. But it was too good to last: *Flying Scotsman's* front end was suddenly wreathed in steam, and the crew had no option other than to shut off steam and coast into the station. It had committed the cardinal sin of failing on the road – a rare occurrence for the 'A3s'. 'If an engine could blush,' said Pegler, '*Scotsman* would have been doing so.'

On shed, it became clear that eight bolts on the back left-hand steam chest had worked loose. It was the work of a saboteur, presumably hell-bent on ensuring that the GWR retained its record. Some railway enthusiasts have particular loyalties, either to companies, or to types of locomotive, and many a lively debate as to their merits or otherwise has taken place, but this was going too far. Pegler's insurance company confirmed the suspicions: the bolts 'had been deliberately slacked off with malicious intent', read its report. Loyalty to a company is one thing, but whoever did this put a national icon at risk and, if the crew hadn't shut off when they did, potentially put passengers in danger.

Pegler was undeterred, and a month later ran a luxury Pullman train from Paddington to Cardiff in aid of the World Wildlife Fund. *Flying Scotsman* carried a jaunty headboard, and the train was colloquially known as 'The Panda Express'. A security guard was placed on her to deter a repeat sabotage attempt, and this time, *Flying Scotsman* was free to run without interruption Driven by ex-GWR driver Williams and fireman Wallis, she reached Swindon in 65 minutes 26 seconds: 10 minutes faster than the GWR's schedule, though the overall record of just less than

Above No. 4472 approaches Peterborough North on 10 April 1965 with a special Pullman train for the staff of Darlington Works after her overhaul there.

Below BR's first generation of passenger carriages were known as Mark 1s. Although not as comfortable or plush as pre-nationalisation types they incorporated a number of technical developments and thousands were built. Today they form the bedrock of most heritage railway fleets.

57 minutes, set in 1932, remained with the GWR. *Flying Scotsman* reached Cardiff in 2 hours 17 minutes, and it's widely reckoned that neither the GWR nor BR was ever able to achieve this with steam.

Throughout 1965 *Flying Scotsman* kept people's attention. Crowd after crowd thronged the lineside for a glimpse. Dozens of schools booked trips behind her, and the Prime Minister, Harold Wilson even got a cab-ride in the locomotive – ironic given that his government was closing railways left, right and centre. By the end of the year, she had more than recouped the £3,000 Pegler paid for her in 1963: not a bad return for an old girl.

But, as 1965 turned to 1966, it was becoming increasingly apparent that depending on continued supplies of coal and water from BR was becoming increasingly precarious. Rapid dieselisation meant that many water towers were being removed, as were the water troughs which enabled a steam locomotive to refresh its tender on the move. To ensure continued operation, Pegler established a separate company called Flying Scotsman Enterprises, and placed the charismatic George Hinchcliffe in charge. To Hinchcliffe fell the task of securing coal and water supplies, and of negotiating with BR to get precious timetable slots – BR had taken the reasonable enough decision that *Flying Scotsman* could only run at a given time if she didn't interfere with scheduled services used by ordinary passengers.

Dealing as a private individual with a giant nationalised company could be extremely difficult, yet there were those in BR who did their very best to help. The Chief Mechanical Engineer of the BR Board, Terry Miller, proved an absolute godsend, offering sound advice, and trying to find a way through the inevitable mass of red tape. This was just as well because as 1966 continued, getting enough water

M81281

to *Flying Scotsman* was proving a real headache. A road tanker was invariably on hand, but pumping it was slow in the extreme – and *Flying Scotsman* could carry something like 4,000 gallons of water without difficulty.

Miller was a far-sighted man, and when Darlington Works was about to close in 1966 he tipped Pegler off that he would need to be self-sufficient in future. He secured a spare boiler and cylinders for *Flying Scotsman* from classmate No. 60041 *Salmon Trout*. With time running out for main line steam, it was a simple case of securing them while he could, and Pegler immediately regarded it as a good acquisition.

Miller also suggested that Pegler could get another tender for *Flying Scotsman* to carry water, connected to her existing tender by a flexible hose. Pegler readily agreed, but stipulated: 'I want a corridor tender, so I can get through!' This would prove easier said than done, as in 1966 the streamlined 'A4' 4-6-2s which carried the last corridor tenders were finally withdrawn. Miller eventually found one, from No. 60004 *Union of South Africa* (a locomotive that would later, thankfully, be preserved), and converted it to

carry just water. The tender cost £1,000, but converting it into a water carrier cost another £6,000 – double the purchase price of the locomotive it was to be hauled by! Nevertheless, it was money well spent, and it ensured that *Flying Scotsman* could run independently of BR's watering facilities.

Flying Scotsman eventually left its small shed at Doncaster station and moved to the town's main depot, Carr. This was extensively converted to diesel operation in 1966, but Pegler used his main line agreement to persuade BR to keep one line open to maintain steam locomotives, complete with pits and the crucial watering and boiler washing-out facilities.

Beeching's insistence that no other operating deals like *Flying Scotsman's* should be concluded meant that by 1967 she was the only privately owned locomotive allowed to run on BR tracks. After Pegler bought *Flying Scotsman*, a number of wealthy individuals, led by Billy Butlin, had brought locomotives from BR, and some, including *Pendennis Castle*, and the Southern Region's *Clan Line* had been used on charter trains. No more! Steam was being eliminated with ruthless haste, and it was only grudging

respect for the letter of Pegler's deal that kept *Flying Scotsman* running. So the tours continued throughout 1967, and, increasingly, *Flying Scotsman* was the only steam locomotive to be seen in many places. Equally, the number of places that she could go to had been steadily diminishing thanks to Beeching's axe (though by now it was Labour's transport secretary Barbara Castle who was doing most of the chopping).

Steam held out on the Southern Region until 1967 with Bulleid's rebuilt 'Merchant Navy' and 'Battle of Britain'/ 'West Country' 4-6-2s holding sway on express services alongside the last handful of the original air-smoothed Bulleid 'Pacifics'. The BR Standards were also able to continue in service with the Southern Region until 1967. Electric trains had been introduced on the Southern Region as early as the 1920s, so it is ironic that it was one of the last to use steam traction on express services. But its policy was straightforward: it wanted to electrify its routes quickly, so why buy diesel trains which would soon be made redundant in any case? As with the other regions, steam was run down during its final years in Southern service, nameplates were removed, number plates disappeared, and a thick coat of grime penetrated every area of the locomotives. Somehow the Southern 'Pacifics' continued to put in impressive performances, regularly reaching speeds of around 100mph on the main line from London to Basingstoke, but nothing could stop the irresistible progress of modernisation.

Below Southern Railway Chief Mechanical Engineer Oliver Bulleid undertook the last attempts at radically improving the steam locomotive with his 'Merchant Navy' 4-6-2s. They incorporated chain driven valve gear enclosed in a lubricating bath and were powerful and free steaming locomotives. Sadly they came too late and were too problematic to prevent steam traction from being eliminated. This is the third of the fleet, No. 21C3, *Royal Mail*.

Opposite Bulleid also developed a smaller version of the 'Merchant Navy' for more lightly laid routes, named after locations in the West Country and people, places and items associated with the Battle of Britain. In 1960 'Battle of Britain' No. 34067 *Tangmere* heads a Dover express near Bromley South, Kent.

NON-STOP SWAN-SONG

9

As 1968 dawned the writing was on the wall. This would be the last year of the steam operation run by British Rail (BR), as British Railways had become known from 1965. Characteristically, Pegler wanted to ensure that it went out with a bang. For years, he'd dreamt of one last non-stop run between London and Edinburgh, and 1 May 1968 was the fortieth anniversary of *Flying Scotsman's* epic run from King's Cross. Pegler badgered, harangued, pestered and pleaded with BR management for the chance to repeat that run, and on 28 February 1968 the Eastern Region's legendary boss, Gerard Fiennes, gave it the green light.

Perhaps it was this that proved the final nail in Fiennes' BR coffin, for he was unceremoniously dumped from office just five days after approving Pegler's ambitious scheme. A month later, to his dismay, but surely to little surprise, Pegler was told that *Flying Scotsman's* last ever non-stop run was off. Frantic negotiations ensued, and, after Pegler offered to bring a £5,000 payment forward, the decision was reversed with just three weeks to go. There wasn't much time to prepare.

If Pegler had left it even a couple of years to try to repeat the epic run, he would have failed. Even with her second tender, there were doubts about whether *Flying Scotsman* could carry enough water to make it without the water troughs that had been used for decades to top up the tenders (via a scoop lowered into the troughs on the move). However, despite seemingly being made redundant by the new diesels, some water troughs were still being used (to top up the steam heating boilers carried by diesels to ensure that passengers stayed nice and warm). There were three sets still in use on the East Coast Main Line, and *Flying Scotsman* would need to make full use of all to stand a chance.

Right At the start of her historic non-stop run to Edinburgh on 1 May 1968 *Flying Scotsman* gets her train under way, with a 'Deltic' diesel next to it.

On 1 May 1968, for the last time, a Gresley 'Pacific' stood at the head of its train at King's Cross waiting for the 10:00 departure time – next stop, Edinburgh. This was high-profile stuff, and the BBC put a film crew on board to record a documentary. Main line steam had less than five months to live, and this was one of the last rites. Nobody wanted to miss it, and King's Cross was once again crowded with onlookers eager to watch steam's final fling.

Pegler was brimming with excitement. Five years after he'd bought *Flying Scotsman*, he looked much the same. He was still a tall, well-built man; the hair was a little thinner, but his moustache was as neatly trimmed as ever, and the fire was still burning in his eyes. Even Pegler was on tenterhooks however: 'I suppose it's like a diver on the high board – now this is happening, I can't wait to get on with it.' Conscious that his agreement with BR still had time to run, he also paid tribute to the nationalised railway:

The objective as far as I'm concerned was to have a go, and it's an extraordinary thing, in my opinion anyway, that on a great nationalised undertaking, one can take out a privately owned piece of machinery forty-five years old and hitch it up to a train of BR stock and take 300 people almost 400 miles on a weekday amid all the other services. Let's face it, this is a pretty sporting gesture by the British Railways Board.

Exactly on time, she pulled away gently from King's Cross, a 'Deltic'-hauled express keeping pace. Gathering speed, she entered the leftmost portal of Gasworks Tunnel, the sound of the diesel clearly audible through the walls. Emerging into daylight just ahead of the 'Deltic', she got her head down and started charging, but imperiously the 'Deltic' overhauled the veteran steam locomotive. It was rather as if the baton had finally, formally and irretrievably, been passed from steam to diesel.

The passengers on the train were a mixed bunch, from lucky young train-spotters, eagerly taking down all the numbers they possibly could, to Captain Holmes and his wife, who were celebrating the fortieth anniversary of the day they met. On 1 May 1928 they had shared a compartment on the very first non-stop run and, in the words of the husband, got on like a house on fire. The wife was initially disappointed to find that there was also a parson in the compartment, but she changed her mind about him when he offered to escort the pair for lunch, allowing them to stay together while still presenting a respectable appearance: in 1928, such things still mattered. They were engaged within three weeks, and were still very much in love forty years on.

Also on the train was the Reverend Wilbert Awdry, who by 1968 was hugely respected as the author of the Thomas the Tank Engine stories. Like many men of the cloth, Awdry

Opposite Driver John Hill and Fireman Raymond Spiller wave to crowds on 1 May 1968.

Right On 14 January 1963 Alan Pegler acknowledges the crowds as he prepares to take *Flying Scotsman* into private ownership.

found himself attracted to the railways, and wanted to mark the occasion in the best way possible. Explaining the appeal of steam, he said simply: 'It's the smell of smoke and the beat of the engine – and the feeling of being pulled not by a mechanical box on wheels, but by something pulsing and alive.'

Hinchcliffe had arranged for a road tanker to be available in case of emergency at Berwick-upon-Tweed, but nobody expected to need it. The first troughs, at Scrooby, were 130 miles from London, and though the water levels seemed low, enough was picked up for the moment. As the train approached Arksey, near Doncaster, disaster almost struck. A broken rail meant a danger signal for *Flying Scotsman*. Pegler, in the cab of *Flying Scotsman*, his sooty-black face glistening with a sheen of sweat, got twitchy, peering over the cab sidesheets to see if the signal had cleared. Crawling at less than walking pace, one of the crew jumped off the engine and ran to the nearest signal telephone to get permission to proceed. Just two seconds before *Flying Scotsman* would have had to stop, the signal turned to green, the crew member climbed up, and she was on her way again. Pegler breathed a sigh of relief: 'It was a damn sight too near for comfort,' he said.

It was like the glory days, when all the top-link express trains were that clean – unlike many of the last remaining passenger trains hauled by steam – and *Flying Scotsman* didn't disappoint. At Wiske Moor, she again picked up

water and continued north. On the approach to Berwick the two locomotive inspectors, whose job it was to ensure the safe operation of the train, were becoming concerned about water levels. With two of the water pick-ups only regarded as average, there was a real possibility that *Flying Scotsman* might run out of water. They held a hurried conference on the footplate, and Pegler, not wanting to influence them, repaired to the buffet car. Still covered in grime, the tension on his face was clear, and his brow was furrowed: 'This is the highly dodgy situation I'd hoped we were not going to find ourselves in.' Pegler guessed that there were between 2,500 and 3,000 gallons in the tenders (a remarkably accurate assessment), and that they would make it without having to stop at Berwick for water. (His mood lightened when somebody pointed out that there were 3,000 bottles of beer on the train: 'I think the old girl would steam very well on light ale!' he beamed.) The decision wasn't his, however: it was down to Chief Locomotive Inspector Les Richards and his deputy George Harland. After their conference, Harland confirmed the good news: 'Inspector Richards and myself consider that with 3,000 gallons of water, we have sufficient to take us to Edinburgh.'

Had *Flying Scotsman* in fact been running low on water, the prearranged plan was for the engine crew to blow their whistle at Lucker, near Berwick, so that the Berwick signalman, who would be listening for it, could prepare for

Below On what is believed to be the last occasion a steam locomotive collected water from water troughs, *Flying Scotsman* looks like she is having an almost perfect pick-up at Danby Whiske on 31 August 1969. The locomotive is ready for her forthcoming visit to America, as witnessed by the bell on her right-hand side.

their arrival. In the event, as she approached Lucker and its vital troughs, the driver spotted a photographer lying on his stomach on the edge of the platform trying to get the definitive shot of the day. There was no option: the driver hung on the whistle to encourage the photographer to get out of the way as the locomotive screamed through the station. Berwick's signalman heard the blast and prepared for the worst, setting the points so that *Flying Scotsman* could go into the goods loop for refreshment. It took much whistling and fist-shaking before *Flying Scotsman's* frantic crew got their countermanding message through to the signalman, and the line was cleared for progress to continue at the last minute.

Flying Scotsman arrived in Edinburgh to a rapturous reception and the sound of bagpipes 30 minutes ahead of the 1928 schedule of 8 hours 15 minutes. Against the bureaucracy of BR, against the determined efforts of a photographer, and against all probability of it ever happening again, she had done it, and repeated history.

Pegler was congratulated by the Mayor of Edinburgh, and on the platforms a crowd ranging from elderly enthusiasts to mothers with young children cheered her arrival. Pegler summed up his feelings: 'I'm very delighted to have done it non-stop,' he said with understated pride – though he must have been bursting with excitement: *Flying Scotsman's* run was a remarkable effort.

As soon as she arrived, Pegler climbed on to the tenders. The rear tender was empty. He moved forward to the front tender, and it was almost empty: the only water *Flying Scotsman* had left was in her boiler. It was that close. Appropriately, Nigel Gresley's beloved daughter Vi was on the train, and afterwards she said: 'I'm so proud. I only wish my father had been here to witness it.' Surely the great man would have been delighted to see his most adored creation prove what she could do one last time.

Three days later, a return non-stop run was attempted, and this time, concerned that the levels in the water troughs were low, one of *Flying Scotsman's* supporters, Terry Robinson, obtained a set of keys to Scrooby troughs and held down the ball-cock to ensure they were full. This time there were no problems, and *Flying Scotsman* was greeted in King's Cross by thousands. But now it really was the end of an era. Hereafter nothing would ever be the same again

10

AMERICAN ADVENTURE

O ne of Pegler's long-held dreams was to show *Flying Scotsman* off to the world by taking her abroad, and particularly to the United States. There had been a long tradition of British locomotives flying the flag across the Atlantic, since the days of the London and North Western Railways' compound *Queen Empress* in 1893. Pegler had a desperate yearning to take a London and North Eastern Railway (LNER) locomotive over the Atlantic – but the opportunity to do so seemed distant.

However, in 1965 the boss of Vermont's Steamtown preservation centre, F. Nelson Blount, met Pegler. The former dive-bomber pilot who owned *Flying Scotsman* and the charismatic, almost evangelical American hit it off immediately. Blount matched Pegler's enthusiasm inch for inch, and when Pegler floated the idea of an American tour, surely over a few drinks, Blount offered to sponsor it. Pegler was flabbergasted, but Blount was serious, and soon Pegler was off to the United States to see if such a trip might be feasible at some point in the future.

Ideas were firmed up, and gradually the idea of using *Flying Scotsman* to lead a trade mission took shape. It was certainly creative thinking, and from 1965 plans slowly developed. Thanks to Blount's generosity, it appeared that a tour would be feasible, both from a technical point of view and, crucially, from a financial one also. With the main line agreement with BR due to expire in 1971, it seemed that after that might be a good time. Pegler's plans, however, were shattered when Blount died in a crash involving his private aeroplane. The sponsor was gone, and the dream was in ashes.

However, Pegler's devil-may-care enthusiasm carried him on. 'Having lost my sponsor,' he said, 'the sensible thing to do would have been to call it off, but by that time I'd become so fired with enthusiasm at the idea of touring America in my own train that I decided to go ahead

Right In August 1969 *Flying Scotsman* approaches Welsh Harp Junction with her US tour train en route from Twickenham to Liverpool.

anyway!' So he formed a new company, *Flying Scotsman* (USA) Ltd, and began to formulate plans. He was given a helping hand by the vice-president of the United States-based Southern Railway (nothing to do with Britain's Southern Railway), W. Graham Claytor. The Southern Railway was celebrating its seventy-fifth anniversary in 1969, and Claytor offered to host the British locomotive, and negotiate for the train to run on five other railways. With such goodwill, Pegler finally set his heart on *Flying Scotsman's* greatest adventure yet.

One thing the train wouldn't be able to do was haul passengers as American laws prevented that. *Flying Scotsman* would, however, be able to haul an exhibition or circus train. With the latter ruled out as being inappropriate and expensive, Pegler opted to run an exhibition train. He had already been approached by a number of businessmen who wanted to showcase their products in the United States, and he thought *Flying Scotsman* would be a great ambassador for Britain, as she was likely to generate goodwill wherever she went. It was typical Pegler: bold and imaginative, and it didn't take long to persuade high-profile names such as Pretty Polly tights, British Petroleum, Lloyds Bank and the Royal Shakespeare Company to offer their backing for the venture. *Flying Scotsman* would be a brilliant gimmick to attract potential buyers to the exhibition, and the fact that it was on a self-contained train would mean that it could be seen by many more people than a static exhibition. It was good thinking, and at the time of 'Buy British', perfectly timed.

It was timed well for the government too, which had decided to present two Pullman carriages used by General Eisenhower and Winston Churchill during the war to the American National Railway Museum in Green Bay, Wisconsin. They could hitch a ride behind *Flying Scotsman*, and would be another popular attraction. Nor were they the only high-profile coaches in the train: an observation car was converted to resemble an English pub (providing a good promotional opportunity for another of the train's supporters, the brewer Watneys) and named 'The Fireman's Rest'. An administration coach was added to the train and five exhibition cars, a mixture of baggage and pigeon coaches Pegler had plucked from the scrap line at York for £200 each. These were painted in chocolate and cream

colours to match the Pullmans, and had a Union Flag at one end, with a Stars and Stripes at the other to reflect the friendship between Britain and America.

The ever-present George Hinchcliffe was to manage the train, after arranging a sabbatical from his teaching job, while BR supplied, at Pegler's expense, drivers Norman Clark of Doncaster and Henry Fosters from Hornsey. Doncaster fireman David Court joined them, as did locomotive inspector Alan Richardson.

It was all coming together, and in anticipation of this, Pegler sent *Flying Scotsman* to the Leeds locomotive builders Hunslet for a major overhaul and replacement of her boiler tubes. These were major jobs now largely beyond the ability of BR works to undertake, as much of the vital equipment needed to overhaul steam locomotives had been disposed of, and those that had the ability lacked the capacity. At Hunslet, inspectors from the United States and Canada (which the tour was also to visit) transport authorities ran the rule over *Flying Scotsman*. Without their approval to run *Flying Scotsman* abroad, all Pegler's plans would come to naught. Hunslet was well-versed in steam locomotives, though, and the officials had nothing to worry about. They gave *Flying Scotsman* their seal of approval and issued her with the precious North American operating permit she would need. Pegler knew that his plans would cause uproar amongst rail enthusiasts and many others. They had come within weeks of losing *Flying Scotsman* earlier in the 1960s, and some were worried about the potential mishaps that could befall this iconic locomotive on her way to the New World. Others worried that she might end up stranded in the United States, perhaps as a tourist attraction, never to return to Britain. Pegler announced the trip while *Flying Scotsman* was still being overhauled in early 1969 and moved immediately to counter the concerns, announcing that, while the tour would run in 1969, *Flying Scotsman* would return to Britain in 1970 and continue to run on BR until the main line contract expired in 1971. After that, he hinted, other foreign tours might be possible, perhaps to Japan and Australia.

Preparations for shipping *Flying Scotsman* moved ahead, and she was given a final fettling up at Doncaster Works in August. There, she was fitted with the brass bell the Americans deemed necessary on the approach to level crossings, and a large hooter on the side of the smokebox, which was rather louder than the classic Gresley whistle fitted above the firebox. She made a test run from Doncaster to Peterborough via Lincoln, and on 31 August 1969 hauled a rail tour from King's Cross to Newcastle for the LNER Society.

Two weeks later, after final preparations, *Flying Scotsman* took its administration coach from Doncaster to Edge Hill depot in Liverpool for the final stage of its journey. The other coaches and exhibition vans had been sent to the

Opposite On 31 August 1969 *Flying Scotsman* was ready for America. The extra whistle and bell were mandatory requirements for the locomotive when approaching level crossings in the United States.

Right In September 1968, the Cunard freight liner *Saxonia* carries No. 4472 *Flying Scotsman*, her two tenders, two Pullman carriages and two double-decker buses, ahead of her trade mission to the United States.

United States a few days earlier: all that remained was for *Flying Scotsman* to join them. Harold Wilson, the Prime Minister, perhaps mindful of the time he'd been on the footplate, offered his blessings to the exhibition.

In September the floating crane *Mammoth* lifted first *Flying Scotsman*, and then her tenders, on to the Cunard freighter *Saxonia*. The imperturbable Pegler admits he had palpitations at the sight of *Flying Scotsman* being lifted like a toy from the dockside: 'Nothing did break, fortunately, but it was certainly a worry: I've never forgotten the sight of it in the air over the ship!'

Her departure was marked with a blaze of publicity. To help promote the train, the famous Scottish pipe-major Robert Crabbe had been recruited to entertain the crowds, as had a group of glamorous young ladies headed by the twenty-one-year-old beauty queen Kathy Leigh, who also acted as Pegler's personal assistant (and became known, inevitably, as 'Miss *Flying Scotsman*'). She and the other girls would act as front-of-house for the exhibition, and provide a welcome glitz to the tour, courtesy of an organisation called London Stateside, which was to sell souvenirs alongside the train in a pair of converted London buses. Furthermore, Sir Winston Churchill's great-nephew, John Spencer Churchill, was to travel with the train to give the Churchillian connection some real-life credibility; he proved a popular travelling companion. With a skirl of pipes and the girls waving goodbye in front of *Flying Scotsman's* smokebox, this fanfare added to the blaze of publicity. She was going to America, and by golly, she was going in the glamour to which she had become so accustomed!

On 28 September Saxonia anchored in Boston harbour after a safe crossing of the Atlantic. Two floating cranes belonging to the US Navy were used to lift *Flying Scotsman*, and with Crabbe piping away, *Flying Scotsman*, her tenders and the administration coaches were unloaded without event. After extensive checks following her sea voyage, *Flying Scotsman* was reunited with the exhibition train on 3 October and undertook a test run from Boston to New London, Connecticut, that day. Ever the opportunist, Hinchcliffe couldn't resist the opportunity to fire her. Inspecting the train the following day, though, he noticed that springs on two of the exhibition carriages were down. Gingerly entering them, he found to his amazement that

Above The ten women who accompanied *Flying Scotsman* to the United States were tasked with selling merchandise and acting as ambassadors for the trade mission. The Bristol Lodekka buses had sales counters on both decks, and were photographed shortly before departure to America in Battersea Park, London.

they were stacked from floor to ceiling with promotional literature. In his memoirs, he recalls a conversation a BR official had with the Port of Boston Authority 'who claimed that the two cars, which on paper, weighed 30 tons each, in fact, according to the crane driver, weighed in at 60 tons! The mystery was solved, but I kept quiet,' he said. That day, she backed into Boston South station to go on parade.

The train was meant to be entirely for business, but the American public had other ideas. Thousands flocked to see her, attracted by the novelty and spectacle of such an unusual sight in their country. Although Britain had just completed the elimination of steam, most of the private railways of the United States had done so long before: 1960 is usually reckoned to be the last significant year of steam operation in the USA, though a number of smaller lines continued beyond then. Furthermore, the rise of the automobile meant that many towns and cities which had once had a rail service were now bereft, their lines, if they hadn't been closed, used exclusively for the gigantic freight trains operated in America. *Flying Scotsman*, then, was a rare sight in every sense.

Hinchcliffe organised it so that the train was free for trade visitors in the mornings and evenings, with the public allowed in during the afternoons. It was a pattern which would work well throughout the tour. But it was another aspect of the tour which worried him: London Stateside seemed hopelessly optimistic. Hinchcliffe did some back-of-an-envelope calculations and realised that this venture, which employed ten girls, would have to take a vast amount to cover its costs.

As the start date of the tour approached, nerves grew: would the reception afforded to her initially be granted everywhere she went, or had America – which that year had landed a man on the moon – advanced too far beyond the steam age to care? There was only one way to find out.

At 07:00 on 12 October *Flying Scotsman* stood at Boston South station, her safety valves simmering with pent-up pressure, and a palpable air of anticipation threaded through the train and amongst the onlookers. American observers, astounded by *Flying Scotsman's* comparatively tiny size, thought she might have problems mounting the grades on her way from Boston to Hartford – and there were worse to come further on in the tour. These concerns weren't helped by a light drizzle that morning, which stood to make the rails as slippery as ice.

Of course, for a locomotive which had hauled far heavier trains during the war, and at speeds far higher than the 50mph maximum imposed throughout the tour, hauling a nine-coach train should be no problem. So it proved. She purred out of the station and on her way south. She surprised the Americans by storming any gradient that could be thrown at her, speed barely slackening in a seemingly effortless demonstration of her power and efficiency. With her burnished apple-green paintwork and glistening, chocolate-and-cream coaches trailing behind, she looked magnificent threading her way through the New England countryside, and perfectly happy in her new environment. She arrived in Hartford later that day and, after overnight servicing, continued to New York. *Flying Scotsman* was going on show in the Big Apple.

And she would go on show in some style. She was to be displayed at the all-electric Penn Station, now underneath Madison Square Gardens (Grand Central would surely have been a more spectacular venue, but this proved impossible to arrange). She was hauled into the station by an electric locomotive to prevent undue pollution, both to comply with local laws and also because the station platforms were underground. She was there for four days, and again, thousands flocked to see her. The tour had got off to a promising start.

Rich Taylor saw her in Penn Station and on her journey from New York:

My impression at the time was that Flying Scotsman *was a prim lady compared with American locomotives.*

Even after I went along the four-track main line to see the train pass, there was little locomotive sound due to the level track and 50mph speed restriction: it wasn't until my first UK trip that I realised British locomotives will match, if not surpass the sound of many of the locomotives here. To this day I find it difficult to believe the train was figuratively speaking in my back yard!

Within days of the tour, though, rumours were circulating that London Stateside wasn't able to pay hotel bills for the girls. Hinchcliffe investigated further: 'It didn't take me long to realise it was impossible to get sufficient numbers of people through the buses to take much more than $100 or so per hour,' he wrote. Hinchcliffe reckoned that getting people in England to part with more than £1 for a souvenir was tricky, but nothing on the buses was under $5, and according to Hinchcliffe, most items were over $10.

The train left New York for Washington D.C. by way of Philadelphia and Baltimore, where a regulator gland failed, as did the brick arch in the firebox, a casualty of the fiercely burning American coal. Worse still, by this point, as Hinchcliffe had feared, London Stateside went bust. It looked as if the girls – a great promotional tool for the train – would be sent home. Hinchcliffe was told that Pegler had taken over the souvenir side, and that the girls would instead work for Flying Scotsman Enterprises (which would operate the locomotive on Pegler's behalf). It was extra work for Hinchcliffe, and he asked if his wife, Frances, could come over to help. Pegler, who recognised the importance of Hinchcliffe to the venture, agreed readily.

The mishaps were recoverable, and the train arrived in the capital on 25 October. Here, the Americans surpassed themselves. So popular was *Flying Scotsman* that crowds queued for more than three hours to inspect the train and see just how differently the British had evolved their steam locomotives.

From Washington D.C., which she left on 28 October, *Flying Scotsman* continued her journey to her hosts, the Southern Railway. Claytor, now president of the railway, was a lifelong steam enthusiast who had kept in working order the mixed-traffic locomotive No. 4051. He'd been planning a special welcome for *Flying Scotsman* in the Deep South: it would be perhaps the most memorable part of the tour.

On 2 November, she steamed towards the medium-sized Alabama city of Anniston. At the same time, Claytor's 'Pacific', No. 4501, hauled a special train from Birmingham, Alabama, and finally the Atlanta Chapter of the National Railway Historical Society sent its preserved freight locomotive, No. 750, to join the other two. It would be a spectacular meeting. The three locomotives and their trains met appropriately at high noon, and after a series of photographic run-pasts, were positioned in a freight yard for display. The difference between British and American practice could not have been starker. Though quite a giant by British standards, *Flying Scotsman* was simply dwarfed by her American counterparts, even though they were only what the Americans would deem medium-sized engines.

Flying Scotsman's pipework was elegantly hidden, and many American enthusiasts used the term 'toy-like' – not in any pejorative sense, but, as Brian Haresnape wrote, 'in amazement that something so fine and delicate of line, so perfect in finish and polish, so model-like in appearance, could actually exist in real life.'

The Americans were stunned, and between 3,000 and 5,000 people flocked to see *Flying Scotsman* that day. Claytor addressed the crowd, whom he told tongue-in-cheek that the Southern would indeed continue to run steam locomotives, but that there was no truth in the scurrilous rumour that it was going to replace its modern diesels with their older counterparts! Pegler loved the occasion, dressed in his overalls and sunglasses, and he

thanked the Southern Railway for hosting *Flying Scotsman* and for finally allowing an LNER locomotive to visit America.

The ceremony over, *Flying Scotsman* continued her journey to Birmingham, and among those treated to a cab ride was the editor of the US enthusiast magazine *Trains*, David P. Morgan. He gushed with enthusiasm: 'One glance at 4472 told one that she was a lady, an accredited member of mechanical high society … every visible inch of her metal bespoke a craftsmanship of construction seldom known in our rough and ready railroading.' It was high praise indeed from a man respected across the USA as an expert.

Reaction across America was almost universally positive – in the town of Cuba, a school class was dismissed early and taken to the tracks to wave at this glamorous foreign train. Elsewhere, enthusiasts travelled thousands of miles to get a glimpse – and, of course, there were many unsuspecting people taken completely by surprise at the sight and sound of a foreign steam locomotive hauling a passenger train through their towns.

For the staff, it must have been an amazing experience. Pegler was feted by the American media, who took immediately to his polished accent and slightly raffish demeanour. They also took to the girls, who found

Above A commemorative cover was issued in 1969 to mark her visit. Below the picture are the names and dates of other British steam locomotives to have visited the United States for exhibition.

Left *Flying Scotsman* departs the depot at Denison, Texas, on 15 June. As with her runs in Britain she drew admiring crowds wherever she went.

themselves a star attraction wherever they went – almost as much as the locomotive! The parties in the observation car of an evening must have been fantastic, with the ever-charismatic Pegler holding forth in the observation saloon, and a ready and seemingly inexhaustible supply of refreshments. It was a once-in-a-lifetime opportunity for everyone, and they made the most of it.

Flying Scotsman and her entourage reached Dallas on 4 November, and then her last tour destination, Houston, on 10 November. The owner, drivers and firemen, as well as the support staff including the ten models, were treated to a civic reception to mark the end of the thirty-nine-day tour. Pegler's last brilliant stunt was to get the astronaut Al Worden to light the fire of *Flying Scotsman* shortly before he flew to the moon on the *Apollo 15* mission. Worden also lit another fire, becoming smitten with Miss *Flying Scotsman* herself, Kathy Leigh. Who says the romance of rail travel is dead?

From Houston, the tour over, *Flying Scotsman* worked the 400 miles to Slaton, Texas, where she and her coaches were stored undercover in a roundhouse for the winter. It was time to take stock: *Flying Scotsman* had been visited, it is reckoned, by 60,000 people, paying $1 each. Many exhibitors had taken substantial orders, and a huge amount of goodwill had been generated, both for *Flying Scotsman* and for Britain. However, it was also an expensive tour to operate, with legal fees and running fees for operating on all but the Santa Fe railroad, and the costs of salaries and staff accommodation – for they all had to be put up in pre-booked motels. Financially, it had only just broken even, but, as Pegler flew home for Christmas, he could justifiably feel pleased with a job well done: so much so that he planned to continue the tour in 1970.

Pegler went to see the Board of Trade, expecting, if not a red carpet, then at least a hearty welcome. He was to be disappointed. 'Their reaction wasn't "Well done old chap; jolly good show for flying the flag," but an extremely lukewarm one, which indicated there would be no further support.' Just as Beeching felt that steam would damage the image of BR, so the Board of Trade now felt that *Flying*

Scotsman would make foreigners think that Britain was an old-fashioned nation which still ran steam locomotives. Even though the Board of Trade was getting requests from companies to be involved, it seemed it was doing its utmost to dissuade them. It looked like the tour would have to be cancelled, and that *Flying Scotsman* would have to return home.

What really persuaded Pegler to try and find a way of making it happen was a major change of heart by the American operating authorities. Though he'd had a few unofficial turns at driving *Flying Scotsman* in America, it was only when he was discussing arrangements for the second tour that a senior official turned to face him and said: 'You own the engine; you'd better drive the goddamn thing!'

Pegler was dumbfounded: 'I couldn't believe my ears,' he admitted: 'After all the red tape on Britain's railways, here was I, a member of the public, being invited to drive a Gresley 'Pacific' at speed for thousands of miles through some of the most majestic scenery in the world!'

For a man like Pegler, there was only one possible thing to do: 'It was my every wish come true, and, although I knew the money was in danger of running out, I said to myself "My God, I'm never going to have this opportunity again, so I'm going to make the most of it for as long as I can and face the music later. If I go broke, I'll just have to work for a living!"'

New displays were organised for the carriages, including, bizarrely, a set of Gilbert and Sullivan models, a collection of original costumes from the British film *Anne of the Thousand Days*, a model railway layout, British textiles, and an exhibit by the Midwest Railways Society of Chicago that was virtually a mobile museum in itself. It was far removed from the big business of the previous year's train.

The plan for the second tour was to run from Slaton, Texas, via Dallas, Fort Worth, Kansas City, St Louis and Chicago, finally arriving in Green Bay for the National Railway Museum on 19 July. One of the Pullman coaches was dropped off there, and *Flying Scotsman* spent a month on display in company with a close cousin – the stream-lined 'A4' 4-6-2 *Dwight D. Eisenhower*, which had been presented by the British government to the museum at the end of steam – moved on into Canada, where she visited a number of cities. She was stored in the huge roundhouse at Spadina, Toronto for the bitter winter.

The tour hadn't passed without mishap. The bearings on one of the Pullman cars, *Isle of Thanet*, ran hot, so it was with some sense of relief that it was dropped off at Green Bay. More seriously, though, the trailing wheels of the locomotive were damaged as it traversed a crossover on its way north. The bearing was damaged severely, and there was no option other than to remove the wheels and machine it. Throughout the blazing-hot afternoon and into the night, the cab-end of *Flying Scotsman* was lifted, and

the wheelset sent to Santa Fe's workshops in Cleburne some 220 miles away at 02:00 the next morning. In a remarkable feat, the repaired wheelset was completed and installed by the end of the following day.

Throughout the second tour, the financial situation became increasingly precarious. Though Hinchcliffe, by now a full-time paid member of the team, tried all his wiles to raise funds, when it came to getting what he called 'dollars that one can actually see and feel', support drained away. Despite this, Pegler revelled in driving his locomotive for mile after mile. It was a childhood dream come true, and he wanted to eke it out as long as he could.

By the time the train reached Ottawa, however, the venture was in trouble. Half the staff were sent home to try and save costs, and worse still, while *Flying Scotsman* was kept securely under cover, the carriages were left outside to weather the harsh Canadian winter. Back in England, the Board of Trade had become the Department of Trade and Industry, and it was adamant that it wasn't going to support what was looking increasingly like a reckless adventure. 'I hope they were satisfied,' said a bitter Pegler, 'because I ended up £132,000 in debt.'

There were real worries now about the future of *Flying Scotsman*, and with good reason. Pegler knew that he would almost certainly become bankrupt, but there was, he felt, the tiniest glimmer of hope. The city of San Francisco was to hold a British Week in 1971, and if *Flying Scotsman* could get there, it was just possible that the commercial situation might be turned around. It was worth a go. Canadian National, which had stored the locomotive over the winter, agreed to release *Flying Scotsman* in return for a percentage of the takings from the journey across America.

Crewing problems reared their ugly head as Pegler tried to keep costs down. He could drive, but for the most part, there just three others for the onerous and demanding footplate tasks. One thing they were never without, though was goodwill, and volunteers galore turned up to help: even doing mundane tasks like cleaning, cooking and taking tickets would lighten the load on the full-time staff. But expertise in operating steam railways was rare in North America, so inevitably much of the burden fell on the British contingent.

AMERICAN ADVENTURE

Opposite Local businesses were quick to capitalise on *Flying Scotsman's* appearances. This hamburger bar is clearly seeking custom from visitors seeing the locomotive at lunchtime at Decateur, Illinois.

From Joliet, on the outskirts of Chicago, to San Francisco, the train's progress became something more like an epic expedition. Photographers, students, industrialists, girls on their way home to California, all became part of the train crew, and all were given regular tasks. Only on the footplate did the professionals (and, of course, Pegler and Hinchcliffe) really hold sway. Getting coal proved another problem. Though the railways on whose tracks *Flying Scotsman* ran did their best to help, all too often they hedged their bets on the financial situation and demanded that the coal was paid for as it was obtained. And the quality got steadily worse as *Flying Scotsman* went further west, with stops to raise steam becoming an irritatingly frequent occurrence. Lack of maintenance facilities also proved a challenge, with much improvisation needed to keep her running: with no ready supply of spares, and using completely different components to American locomotives, *Flying Scotsman's* survival depended on her reliability.

Kevin Bunker was just one of many US rail enthusiasts compelled to go trackside to welcome 4472 to Northern California and the Bay Area. He was about sixteen at the time, but more than thirty-five years on, it left a vivid impression with him:

I had not, until that moment, seen live mainline steam of any kind, having been born just before Southern Pacific Company dropped the fires in the last of its steam power in the later 1950s. It seemed a bit odd, to be sure, that a three-cylinder Gresley 'Pacific' from the UK on the Western Pacific Railroad (of all roads) would be my first experience, but there you are.

Joining several friends from the Bay Area, we chased south from Sacramento (my hometown) to see 4472 leave the South Sacramento yards, which was rather underwhelming. Figuring we could not catch it anywhere on the way to Stockton, we simply dashed all the way to the latter city and waited trackside for the special train to approach the Santa Fe Railway-Western Pacific diamond crossing. In due course, 4472 and train made its way into Stockton, its borrowed Southern Railway brass chime whistle announcing its passage across the numerous level crossings along the way.

She was moving so slowly due to the crowds around the passenger depot that we continued to be surprised that the locomotive seemed to lack 'presence' – a throaty voice at the chimney, if you will. Of course, we still had not yet seen the engine really work, let alone sprint at track speed. Suddenly, 4472 was given clearance to cross another line and she burst forward with the distinctive Gresley loping exhaust. Those far older than me who recalled Southern Pacific's Alco 4-10-2s would have remembered that off-centre exhaust beat, but it certainly surprised my ears!

I hoped to see 4472 operating in San Francisco on the port railroad, but on the one day I did visit, she was on static display. On that occasion, though, I managed to get a few minutes with Alan Pegler in the former 'Devon Belle' observation car, after which, he conducted me through the train and the corridor tenders up into 4472's footplate and cab. I was a budding railway artist in those years, and brought as a gift a recent sketch I'd made of a West Side Lumber Company Shay locomotive – a curious choice on my part, but which utterly charmed Alan, who from that moment became a friend. We corresponded off and on for some years until he retired to Wales, after which we lost touch.

Bunker's enthusiasm is a typical illustration of the lengths rail enthusiasts will go to pursue their passion, and he wasn't alone. Many American railroad fans flocked to the lineside to witness this foreign locomotive speed past.

As the end of September 1971 approached, *Flying Scotsman* and her train were given a refresh to prepare them for British Week, and on 27 September she finally arrived at Fisherman's Wharf in San Francisco. At this point, control was handed over to Flying Scotsman Enterprises to try and make enough money to repatriate this iconic locomotive. Fisherman's Wharf was just long enough for a seven-coach train, so one of the windowless exhibition cars had been left behind en route. Things were now getting really desperate financially, with the staff sleeping aboard the train and, every three or four nights, a motel room being hired. The crew took it in turns to use the shower and wash their socks and underwear. A different person would sleep in the room each night, chosen by a rota.

Pegler was being chased by creditors, and at one point, a writ was even slapped on *Flying Scotsman's* buffer beam. Pegler ripped it off, but it was a near thing. Promised sponsorship had failed to materialise, and as a final punch in the face, although the authorities were prepared to let *Flying Scotsman* stay on Fisherman's Wharf for six months, they would only do so if they were compensated for the loss of revenue from the ninety-three parking meters it occupied. It cost Pegler £1,000 per week, but amazingly, she made a profit, so great were the crowds wanting to walk through the train and corridor tender. One unusual visitor was the singer Tom Jones, then at the height of his fame, and for six months from September 1971, *Flying Scotsman* was one of the most popular tourist attractions, if not the most popular, in a city not short of them.

The train became a popular venue for business meetings, corporate entertaining and social functions, and if she had been allowed to remain there, it seems likely that enough money would have been made to pay off Pegler's debts and repatriate the locomotive. However, the local businesses on Fisherman's Wharf felt they were losing business because there was nowhere for potential customers to park, and

Flying Scotsman was ordered to move to the other end of the quay.

This initially seemed like a good move, because after much negotiation with safety authorities, Hinchcliffe and Pegler won permission to operate 2-mile shuttle trips on the San Francisco Belt Railroad, making *Flying Scotsman* the first and only British train to carry fare-paying passengers on a US railway. This started off well and, with fares priced at $3 return, seemed to make money, but it soon proved a false dawn. Speed was limited to just 10mph, thanks to all the level crossings and the constant bell-ringing the locomotive had to do, and the smoke and noise soon caused complaints from locals. But the final nail in the coffin was that *Flying Scotsman* was out of the public eye. The spontaneous tourist trade evaporated, and within just a few weeks of the first run on 14 March, Pegler was staring bankruptcy straight in the face.

Although he could have stayed in the US and avoided it, because his son Tim was a permanent resident of the US, Pegler opted to return to Britain to sort out his, and the locomotive's future. He was bought a return ticket by one of *Flying Scotsman's* American supporters and, after filing for bankruptcy in July 1972, he returned to see what could be done to save his beloved engine. For *Flying Scotsman*, it was as dark an hour as in January 1963, when she had been due to be withdrawn by BR. This time, though, there was no knight in shining armour waiting in the wings.

Hinchcliffe came to the fore and arranged for *Flying Scotsman* and her train to be stored at the Sharpe Army Depot: a place creditors would find hard to enter, and one which offered secure storage. In light steam, and hauled by a diesel, she left San Francisco on 13 August 1972. As the crew put *Flying Scotsman* to bed and disbanded, it looked as if the fires had gone out forever. Hinchcliffe resumed his career in teaching, and Pegler, financially ruined by the engine he had done so much to save and keep running, sat down on Fisherman's Wharf, scratched his head, and said: 'What on earth do I do now?'

Above Enthusiasts in the United states were keen to see No. 4472 in full cry and as *Flying Scotsman* crosses Interstate 70 she makes a fine spectacle on a beautiful day.

RESCUE

While Alan Pegler sat on Fisherman's Wharf in San Francisco pondering his next move, concern was growing in Britain about the fate of *Flying Scotsman*. By a cruel irony, three of *Flying Scotsman* Enterprises' principal creditors were railway companies. There was to be no solidarity with their British debtor. *Flying Scotsman* was the principal asset,

and they, and the other creditors, wanted to recover as much of their costs as possible.

It didn't take long for momentum to build up in Britain to save it, led by Alan Bloom, one of the pioneering railway preservationists. Bloom, a horticulturalist, ran Bressingham Gardens in Norfolk, and was busy establishing a railway centre as an added attraction. He had bought some small

Below On 14 February 1973 *Flying Scotsman* awaits unloading at Liverpool Docks from SS *California Star*. The locomotive would have to have a detailed examination before she could potentially run to Derby for overhaul under her own power.

tank engines, but he also had custodianship of British Rail's (BR) last steam locomotive to haul a passenger train, the 'Britannia' 4-6-2 *Oliver Cromwell*. He formed a committee to try and repatriate *Flying Scotsman*, and one of his first acts was to call his friend, and fellow locomotive-owner, William McAlpine, of the construction company.

McAlpine, then in his thirties, had long been a steam enthusiast and, after a spell of national service in the 1950s, had continued to work his way through the ranks of the McAlpine company. He had bought *Flying Scotsman's* great rival, *Pendennis Castle*, with Lord Gretton and was also starting to build up a collection of steam traction engines and locomotives at his home in Buckinghamshire. He was well off, and might be in a position to help the public appeal to save *Flying Scotsman* that was envisaged.

Over the years McAlpine has acquired a large and magical collection of railway artefacts widely reckoned to be the biggest collection outside the National Railway Museum, and it encompasses a number of sheds full to the rafters of everything from furniture to signs, to models and nameplates. Best of all, though, is the railway in the grounds of his house. Sir William has built from new a running line of around a mile in length complete with stations, signal box and level crossing. The locomotive, a small saddle tank, was the last steam locomotive used by the family firm, Sir Robert McAlpine.

Before the committee set up to bring *Flying Scotsman* home could do much, however, shocking news came from the United States: three railway companies which were creditors were working together to try and seize *Flying Scotsman* and her coaches to sell for as much money as possible. Action was needed urgently, and as soon as he found out, Bloom called McAlpine: 'Alan Bloom gave me a ring to say, "We are here, and *Flying Scotsman's* in trouble. We think we ought to get together and do something." And I said, "Well the only thing to do is get hold of George Hinchcliffe,"' recalls McAlpine.

Although Hinchcliffe was now back teaching, McAlpine, who had seen *Flying Scotsman* in San Francisco, knew well that he was the best person to sort things out. McAlpine agreed to pay Hinchcliffe's fare to Washington D.C. to meet the lawyers and waited patiently for him to get back in touch. Hinchcliffe arrived on 30 December 1972 and called the lawyer Bill Mann. Mann gave him the bad news that the creditors were now actively seeking the court order that would give them custody of *Flying Scotsman*. He was sceptical of McAlpine (though when he learned that McAlpine was born in London's Dorchester Hotel, he became more reasonable). The railway creditors were unwilling to allow more time for a deal to be sorted, so McAlpine and Hinchcliffe would have to work quickly.

McAlpine asked Hinchcliffe if he could arrange the move back to Britain, and Hinchcliffe said yes. By an incredible

coincidence, Hinchcliffe had sat next to a man who worked for a shipping line in San Francisco called Johnson Scanstar. Hinchcliffe explained his problems, told him where he could be located in San Francisco (where he had flown to see friends) and never really expected to hear from him again. To his surprise, there was a message awaiting him after a meeting: 'I have a ship sailing in fourteen days – please phone.' Hinchcliffe did, and he agreed a price before calling McAlpine to confirm that he could arrange *Flying Scotsman's* shipment home.

McAlpine hesitated before asking his second question: 'If you get it back, will you run it for me and manage it?' Hinchcliffe replied that he would have to ask his wife Frances, but she readily agreed. 'With that, all I could say was "yes",' thought McAlpine. The funds were transferred in the nick of time for just half the amount the railroads

wanted: finally, it looked as if *Flying Scotsman's* future was secure – although Hinchcliffe remained twitchy about some hitherto unknown creditor suddenly appearing.

Western Pacific Railroad was understandably reluctant to get involved with *Flying Scotsman* once more, but, after the promise of payment in advance, agreed to move her from Sharpe Army Depot to San Francisco Docks, where she would be lifted on to barges, and then on to the ship that was to take her home, the *California Star*. To Hinchcliffe's horror, it now appeared that the San Francisco Port Authority was one of the creditors: was everything to fall apart at the last minute? 'Here we were right in the lion's den, and, to make things worse, we had a reporter anxious to catch the evening's edition!' he remembers.

There was only one thing to do with a nosy reporter: ply him with scotch. Hinchcliffe made sure the reporter was so drunk there was no way he could file copy, and, once *Flying Scotsman* was safely, securely and irrecoverably loaded, he went to meet Pegler (who was still in San Francisco) and give him the good news: *Flying Scotsman* was coming home, with her second tender – but the coaches and exhibition vans would be left behind.

McAlpine was the one person in Britain in a position to save *Flying Scotsman*, given the time constraints imposed by the American creditors. His generosity – and, crucially, his decisiveness – ensured that, rather than ending up stuffed and mounted at somewhere like Long Beach, home of such retired transport icons as the liner *Queen Mary* and the 'Spruce Goose' flying boat (this was a real possibility at the time), the locomotive would have a future in Britain. He soon bought it from Pegler for what Pegler calls 'a song', and then *Flying Scotsman* was his to do whatever he wanted with. Intriguingly, a very short article was published in *The Railway Magazine* after the deal had been sealed, saying that the locomotive was to be donated to the National Collection. Given McAlpine's desire to see *Flying Scotsman* running, and for George Hinchcliffe to manage it, one wonders whether this was mere journalistic wishful thinking. Certainly, nothing more was heard of this plan. It didn't matter: McAlpine's sound business sense meant that there was to be no repeat of the American adventure.

The journey from San Francisco to Liverpool via the Panama Canal was a rough one. The *California Star* was hit by the terrifying force of an Atlantic gale, but thankfully, *Flying Scotsman* had been extremely securely fastened to the deck, and survived without damage. She arrived back at Liverpool on 13 February 1973 to a rapturous reception. The floating crane unloaded her, and McAlpine sat on the fireman's seat: 'This engine is mine – I don't believe it! I never really felt like I owned her,' he confided.

Now that she had landed in Britain, McAlpine intended to send *Flying Scotsman* to BR's Derby Works for a much-needed overhaul. It was hoped that she could make the journey under her own steam, but in order for that to happen, BR needed to be sure that storage in America

and the sea voyage hadn't left her unfit for service. She certainly looked work-stained, but that would mean little to BR's diligent inspectors, all of whom remembered steam well. They were satisfied she would be fine to continue – and in fact, she still had some really high-quality coal from Utah in her tender – but the final decision was up to the regional manager, Dick Hardy. Hardy was one of the greatest operating men ever to work on the railways, and he was also an out-and-out steam man. There was no way he would refuse permission for *Flying Scotsman* to run to Derby under her own steam if his inspectors agreed that she was in good enough condition to make it: it was a momentous decision.

Once again *Flying Scotsman* was headline news, as amidst euphoria she steamed proudly to Derby. It was like a royal visit, with the lineside all the way thronged with well-wishers overjoyed to see her back. A flight of Royal Air Force Phantom fighter-bombers even saluted her as she steamed eastwards. The only thing missing was the sound of church bells ringing to mark the homecoming.

Opposite *Flying Scotsman's* tender was unloaded first, still with American coal inside. She would use some of it on her run to Derby for overhaul.

Below Despite being stored in America locomotive inspectors passed *Flying Scotsman* fit to travel to Derby under her own steam. In February 1973 the locomotive arrives in Derby to cheers from waiting crowds.

At Derby, *Flying Scotsman* had her American accoutrements taken off. The unsightly hooter and headlamp bracket were removed, as was the bell. She was stripped down and emerged repainted in the apple green that suited her so well. She was launched – and what a change of heart this demonstrated – by BR's Chairman, Richard Marsh, before heading to her new home in Devon.

BR's steam ban which meant that other than *Flying Scotsman*, no other steam locomotives were able to operate on the national network, had proved short-lived.

One of the National Collection's most popular steam locomotives, the Great Western Railway's (GWR) gigantic 4-6-0 *King George V*, had been kept in steam by the cider makers Bulmers in Hereford, where she hauled short demonstration trains on the company's sidings. Peter Prior of Bulmers wanted to use the locomotive on a promotional train, and after lengthy negotiations, in October 1971 – the year Pegler's agreement with BR expired – *King George V* was on a special train which included a couple of carriages for fare-paying passengers. The run was a massive success,

Opposite Another of the very earliest standard-gauge railways to be preserved was the Bluebell Railway from Sheffield Park to Horsted Keynes and ultimately East Grinstead. Amongst its early supporters was actress Avril Gaynor, who helped restore 'P' 0-6-0T No. 323 *Bluebell* in the 1960s. The locomotive is operational today, and is typical of the small steam locomotives generally acquired by those early heritage railways.

Below The North Yorkshire Moors Railway was one of the first generation of heritage railways, and over the years it has grown into a tourist attraction of immense importance, carrying hundreds of thousands of passengers a year. This is the pretty station of Goathland with British Rail (BR) Standard '4MT' 2-6-0 No. 76079 preparing for departure.

and, having seen the goodwill it generated, BR relented. The steam ban was over, just three years after the end of main line steam operation. There were caveats – steam operation was banned in the summer because of the fire risk, and just six short routes were cleared – but it was a start, and it meant that the giants of steam would be able to stretch their legs properly.

By the time *Flying Scotsman* emerged from Derby it was July 1973, which meant that she wouldn't be able to earn her crust on the main line as it was summer. However, while she had been in America, something truly remarkable had happened that meant that whatever the policy regarding main line steam, there would always be a railway for *Flying Scotsman* to run on: the railway preservation movement was building up a head of steam that continues to this day.

The Beeching cuts of the 1960s were so extensive that in many cases, lines were closed and simply allowed to rot rather than being demolished, and that gave a brief window of opportunity to resurrect old lines. In the 1950s the Ealing comedy *The Titfield Thunderbolt* had made fun of the idea of a bunch of eccentrics trying to keep their line open, but by the late 1960s and early 1970s the notion was widespread enough for ridicule to evaporate. An idea hitherto restricted by sheer practicality to the narrow-gauge railways of Wales suddenly exploded into reality on the standard-gauge lines of England, Wales and Scotland. The first was the Middleton Railway in Leeds at the end of the

left It was a Great Western Railway (GWR) locomotive that broke BR's infamous 'steam ban' after 1968. On 2 October 1971, No. 6000 *King George* V approaches Llanvihangel whist running from Hereford to Tyseley on the first stage of her return to steam special with the Bulmer Cider Pullmans.

1758 Middleton Railway Leeds

The world's oldest railway

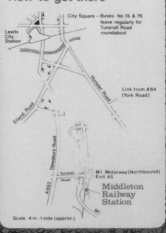

Bagnall Engine
'Matthew Murray'
Type 0 4 0 ST
Built in 1943

Timetable

Scale 4 in : 1 mile (approx.)

M1
Exit 45

Works

British Rail Line

Works

Halt

Works

M1

G.N.R. Route
(disused)

Halt

Middleton Woods
Café, Boating,
Ideal picnic spot

Steam Trains
run every
Saturday and
Sunday afternoon,
and also on
Bank Holidays
between Easter
and the end
of September,
between 14.00 & 16.30

A half hourly
service is normally
maintained

Fares
Adult single
Child single

The Middleton Railway

The present Middleton Railway is the
direct descendant of the Middleton
Wagon Way, authorised by an Act of
Parliament in 1758 to take coal from
the Middleton Colliery to Leeds.
1812 saw the first successful commercial
use of steam locomotives in the world.
Since 1960 the line has been preserved, and the Middleton Railway has
acquired a selection of industrial locomotives (steam and diesel) to haul
both passenger and freight trains.

MEMBERSHIP of the Middleton Railway brings free
train rides, an illustrated magazine and a chance to help
in the work of preserving this historic line.

ADDRESS for all enquiries :

MIDDLETON RAILWAY
GARNETT ROAD
LEEDS LS 11 5JY

How to get there

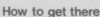

City Square – Buses No 74 & 76
leave regularly for
Tunstall Road
roundabout

Leeds
City
Station

Link from A64
(York Road)

Hunslet Road

Elland Road

Dewsbury Road

Tunstall
Road

A683

M1 Motorway (Northbound)
Exit 45

Middleton
Railway
Station

M1

Scale 4 in : 1 mile (approx.)

1950s, closely followed by the Bluebell Railway in Sussex, but it was really from the mid-1960s that some of the most famous names in railway preservation got going. The North Yorkshire Moors Railway from Grosmont to Pickering; the Keighley and Worth Valley Railway; the Severn Valley Railway; what is now called the Dartmouth Steam Railway – all had their genesis in the 1960s, and by 1973 all were carrying passengers. There were others too, in varying states of completion.

A number of wealthy individuals and groups had bought engines directly from BR: mostly big express types, but also mixed-traffic types including a former London and North Eastern Railway 'B1', and a number of the steadfast 'Black Fives' introduced by the London, Midland and Scottish Railway in the 1930s. These provided some of the motive power for the embryonic heritage railways, as did industrial locomotives bought from companies upgrading to diesel traction. The biggest spur of all, though, came from a forgotten scrapyard in Wales.

In the 1960s the scrap merchant Dai Woodham bought hundreds of steam locomotives, carriages and wagons from BR. He concentrated on the carriages and wagons first, as they were easier to break up, and, as business was good, he was content to leave the steam locomotives to gently rust away until a quieter time. It didn't take long for word to get out amongst enthusiasts that there were something like 200 steam locomotives in a scrapyard in Barry, and it didn't take long either for groups to start buying them from Woodham and begin the lengthy process of restoration. This combination of closed lines and a ready (at a price) source of motive power really secured the future of railway preservation at a time when some wondered about its appeal.

McAlpine decided to send *Flying Scotsman* to run on the Dartmouth Steam Railway (to use today's name) for the summer season of 1973 after her overhaul at Derby. The line runs from Paignton to Kingswear in glorious Devon. She hauled McAlpine's immaculate pair of inspection saloons from Derby without difficulty, and settled in to a ten-week season hauling tourist trains on this picturesque little line, doing five return trips daily for four days a week. She

proved a huge attraction, both with passengers and staff. There was, almost inevitably, some friendly regional rivalry between the GWR loyalists of the Torbay Steam Railway and *Flying Scotsman's* own crew. One day she was rostered to haul a thirteen-coach train from Paignton, assisted by the GWR 'Manor' *Lydham Manor*. *Flying Scotsman's* supporters claimed the locomotive would take the coaches and *Lydham Manor* single-handed. The *Manor's* crew said their engine could do the same in the opposite direction. The gauntlet was laid down, and without further ado, *Flying Scotsman* strolled away with her train, probably equivalent to something like fifteen coaches with the added dead weight of *Lydham Manor*. At the steepest point on the line, the safety valves started to lift, sure proof that *Flying Scotsman* had plenty in hand.

On the return journey, *Lydham Manor* gamely struggled with her heavy load, but as the speed came down to just 10mph, her crew had to finally acknowledge that they needed help from the bigger engine if they were to keep time. Game, set and match to *Flying Scotsman*, albeit against a much smaller and less powerful engine.

As summer turned to autumn, main line steam again became practical, and on 22 September *Flying Scotsman* teamed up with *King George V* to haul a train from Newport to Shrewsbury. The train was appropriately named 'The Atlantic Venturers Express', and it was the first time that two British locomotives that had visited America hauled the same train. The reception involved the usual crowds: anyone who wondered whether *Flying Scotsman* really was back and on form knew for certain now! The pair savaged the steep gradients on this line, making them appear almost as if they weren't there: these were two locomotives on the very top of their game.

Because *King George V* was too wide and tall for some routes, *Flying Scotsman* was used to haul the Bulmers promotional train in the north of England. Of course, her corridor tender meant that when she was on display, people could enter her cab, and then walk through the corridor tender to the train. She was as popular as ever, but McAlpine and Hinchcliffe knew that the present ad hoc arrangements would have to be replaced by something more permanent. *Flying Scotsman* was moved to a shed at Market Overton near Grantham on a branch line serving an iron-ore quarry, where McAlpine's other big engine, *Pendennis Castle*, was maintained. It was appropriate the two locomotives should be stabled together given their shared history. The pair worked a number of rail tours together, and on runs between Newport and Shrewsbury *Flying Scotsman* proved just how much more efficient the higher-pressure boiler and better valves fitted in 1947 were. Even though she had to haul her second tender, her coal consumption was less than *Pendennis Castle's*: 8 per cent less, according to Hinchcliffe.

THE STORY OF BARRY SCRAPYARD

BR offered selected scrap merchants the work of scrapping withdrawn steam locomotives when their own works were unable to cope, and amongst them was Woodham Brothers Ltd of Barry, South Wales. The first batch of locomotives arrived in 1959 but Woodham Bros. was also involved in scrapping withdrawn carriages and wagons as well as old rails. These were easier to scrap and so the locomotives sat in the yard waiting their turn. In August 1968, when BR withdrew its last steam locomotive, there were more than 200 steam locomotives awaiting scrapping at Barry Docks and the scrapyard began to draw the attention of railway enthusiasts who started to acquire them. From this beginning grew the bedrock of the heritage railway movement. In total 213 steam locomotives were rescued from Barry Scrapyard and without the decision by yard owner, Dai Woodham (awarded an MBE in 1997), to delay scrapping them many would have been lost forever.

Above Welsh scrap merchant Dai Woodham saved hundreds of steam locomotives from being scrapped when his workforce ran out of easier to dispose material. Almost all of them from the early 1970s were saved by preservationists. In the 1960s and 1970s it was like an elephant's graveyard for steam engines.

Difficulties in extracting the iron ore at Market Overton meant that the mine's closure was inevitable, but it was only when BR wanted to ease the curve on the main line at High Dyke to allow higher speeds, and demanded £100,000 to reinstate the connection to the Market Overton branch that McAlpine and Hinchcliffe decided they had to move *Flying Scotsman* and *Pendennis Castle*. The location they chose was the old steam shed at Carnforth, Lancashire. Carnforth was, and is, unique: it was operational on the last day of BR steam in 1968, and is probably the last 'modern' steam depot in the country. Its gigantic coaling stage and comprehensive facilities made it an ideal base for the burgeoning main line steam movement. It was also close to the Cumbrian Coast line and the lines from Leeds to Carnforth and from Guide Bridge to Sheffield – three of the few lines steam was allowed to operate on – and therefore made an ideal base for *Flying Scotsman* and her ilk.

Meanwhile, BR was extending permission to operate steam locomotives on the national network only on a yearly basis, something that McAlpine was increasingly concerned about, given the high cost of overhauls and maintenance. So he took BR's Chairman, Sir Robert Reid for lunch and in his usual diplomatic way, made the case for a longer period of steam operation than a year. McAlpine offered to form an association of steam locomotive owners who wanted to run their locomotives on the main line which would deal directly with BR. In doing this he floated an idea which seems to have come from the ever-inventive mind of Hinchcliffe: a kind of co-operative among steam locomotive owners to divide the main line work there was, and to form a single point of contact between the owners and BR. It became known as the Steam Locomotive Owners' Association (SLOA), and it was to prove highly successful.

With main line steam now virtually guaranteed a secure future on BR, the work continued for *Flying Scotsman*, and she was an ever-popular draw. In 1976 she was led by the venerable London and North Western Railway 2-4-0 express passenger engine *Hardwicke* – some fifty years older than *Flying Scotsman* – over the picturesque Settle to Carlisle line to mark the route's centenary. Filming appearances in disguise ensured 1977 was interesting to her supporters, and after an overhaul by Vickers at Barrow-in-Furness, where she was fitted with her spare boiler, she hauled two special trains in memory of the great railway photographer, the Rt Revd Eric Treacy, the Bishop of Wakefield, who died on Appleby station while watching his beloved steam locomotives. *Flying Scotsman* was an appropriate locomotive, and the commemorations were well-received, both by BR and the public.

Amazingly, that year, BR decided to resume operation of steam *itself*. It hired *Flying Scotsman* to work the Cumbrian Coast Express, a special train aimed at holidaymakers in the area, from Carnforth to Sellafield and back. Sellafield might not have been the most obvious destination, but the scenery is beautiful, and there was a miniature railway, the Ravenglass and Eskdale, too. The trains proved highly popular, but only ran for two years.

Flying Scotsman had a steady workflow and a wealthy backer determined to run her as a business rather than an indulgence, as reflected by the fact that – unlike Pegler, who took every opportunity to travel behind her – McAlpine remained dedicated to his family business. That didn't stop the Inland Revenue chasing McAlpine to try and extract more money from him, however: 'The tax people tried to prove that it was a hobby, so that any losses *Flying Scotsman* incurred wouldn't be set against income tax.' It was a reasonable enough concern, but they made too many unwarranted assumptions: surely the owner of *Flying Scotsman* would be on it all the time – wouldn't he? McAlpine proved that, in that particular year, he had travelled behind *Flying Scotsman* just three times. After all, as he points out: 'I was working and the job came first, and my family came first as well.' And *Flying Scotsman* was doing extremely well with Hinchcliffe and the dedicated support crew behind it. 'I've never been particularly excited by driving it,' says McAlpine. 'I would much rather sit in the saloon at the back and hear the sounds and take in the smell. Actually I want to see the thing properly.'

As the 1970s turned into the 1980s, *Flying Scotsman* continued her main line and occasional promotional work, and, as it saw the benefits of main line steam, BR gradually widened the number of routes steam locomotives were allowed to operate on. In 1983, to mark *Flying Scotsman's* sixtieth anniversary, she was exhibited at the National Railway Museum in York, and the following day travelled solo to Doncaster and then to Peterborough to haul a special train back to York. It was a time of celebration, but it almost marked the end for main line steam. As *Flying Scotsman* approached Stoke Bank, near Grantham, some of the crowd thronging the lineside encroached on to the line to get a better view, or more likely, picture. It was stupid and dangerous. And things were to get worse further north. Having negotiated Grantham without incident, *Flying Scotsman* approached Newark eagerly. Very soon however, the crowds got out of control, thronging on to the East Coast Main Line – a line with a maximum speed in places of 125mph. The police in attendance had little choice: for the trespassers' own safety, they were forced to close the line for 15 minutes to clear the crowd. This caused disruption to other trains and placed railway staff and the police themselves at risk. BR's management was understandably concerned, and its Chairman, Bob Reid, issued stern instructions that this must not happen again. For the moment, steam was on probation. It was tribute to *Flying Scotsman's* popularity that so many people wanted to see her – but the irresponsible actions of a few placed main line steam under a considerable cloud, for a while at least. It would not be the last time this would happen.

Flying Scotsman was allowed to continue operations, and paid a visit to Scotland, where she was adopted by a Territorial Army regiment who placed a guard round her at Eastfield depot. After exhibition at Glasgow Queen Street, she visited Perth and Edinburgh, crossing the Forth Bridge, where she had been so brilliantly captured on canvas by Terence Cuneo.

Flying Scotsman's fame was such that when the Queen Mother opened the North Woolwich Station Museum in London the locomotive hauled the Royal Train. Flying Scotsman was burnished to perfection, and when, on the footplate, the Queen Mother was told the locomotive had been built in 1923, she commented wistfully: 'That was the year I was married.' The Royal Train was a huge success, and sealed Flying Scotsman's official approval.

In 1985 Flying Scotsman was due for another overhaul to remain running on the main line. By this time, BR had devised a thorough-going policy to regulate the operation and maintenance of steam locomotives. Once insurance inspectors had confirmed that a locomotive met BR's high standards and the boiler was first steamed (even if it had yet to be fitted to the locomotive itself), a clock started ticking.

Above In 1974 *Flying Scotsman* was based at Steamtown Carnforth, a former BR Motive Power Depot in use until the last year of main line steam operation and perfectly located for the fledgling main line operations. Now owned by Sir William McAlpine, she would stretch her legs once more on main line metals. She stands next to Stanier 'Black Five' 4-6-0 No. 45407.

Left On 14 September 1975 *Flying Scotsman* crosses Plawsworth Viaduct on her old East Coast Main Line stamping ground. The scene has changed significantly with electrification.

left Gradually BR expanded the routes that steam locomotives could operate on, coming to the view that *Flying Scotsman* and other preserved engines 'warmed the market' for railways. On 12 January 1986 – Sir William McAlpine's birthday – No. 4472 leaves her old stamping ground of London Marylebone with the 'Half Century Limited' to Stratford-upon-Avon.

It was given what is known as a boiler certificate to prove it was safe to operate. After ten years, the boiler would have to be removed from the locomotive and completely overhauled, but, in view of the fact that operating at high-speed on the main line was far more demanding than the 25mph maximum allowed on heritage railway, BR stipulated that at the end of seven years on the boiler certificate, it would have to be overhauled and recertified in order to run on the main line – although the owner of the locomotive could, if he or she wanted, use the remaining three years of the boiler certificate on preserved lines if desired.

A key figure was appointed at this time to help keep *Flying Scotsman* running. Roland Kennington was an experienced engineer, and ultimately became engineer-in-charge in 1986. Little could he have suspected just how long he would be involved with *Flying Scotsman* back then! Two days before Christmas 1985, while working at Bedford engineering company W.H. Allen, he received a phone call from *Flying Scotsman's* groom, Ray Towell. Part of the valve gear had snapped in two, and, knowing of Kennington's experience with 'A4' 4-6-2 *Sir Nigel Gresley*, Towell decided to see what W.H. Allen could do. With the works closed for ten days over Christmas, Kennington said that the best he could do was to weld the part back together. Towell agreed and sent it to Bedford first on a train to Milton Keynes, and thence by taxi. Kennington's work meant that BR allowed *Flying Scotsman* to make two

journeys with it, and the special trains planned to mark the fiftieth birthday of *Flying Scotsman's* owner William McAlpine ran satisfactorily.

Four months later, Kennington was called by the head of SLOA, and the man in operational charge of *Flying Scotsman*, Bernard Staite. He told Kennington that McAlpine wanted to move *Flying Scotsman* from Carnforth and the team that was looking after her. Kennington thought that the broken part of the valve gear (which had been caused by a bolt left in the motion during the overhaul) was a contributory factor. McAlpine wanted the locomotive cared for by a group of volunteers, with Kennington as honorary chief engineer. After careful consideration, Kennington decided he could fit *Flying Scotsman* in with his day job and family commitments and readily agreed.

From Carnforth, it was decided to move *Flying Scotsman* south to London's Marylebone station, where a number of special steam-hauled trains to Stratford-upon-Avon called 'The Shakespeare Express' were to run. Marylebone was that rare thing: a station with an operational turntable on which the locomotives could turn round easily. London's terminus stations were new ground for main line steam in the 1980s, and the first locomotive to break it was, appropriately, 'A4' 4-6-2 No.4498 *Sir Nigel Gresley*, which had first been unveiled in front of her designer at Marylebone in November 1937.

Flying Scotsman took her turns on the Shakespeare Express, returning to the station to which Ken Issitt and Cyril Chamberlain had nursed her after her almost final journey in the early 1950s. It was a happy reunion, and Flying Scotsman proved an extravagantly able performer on the train. She seemed happy in the capital, and in view of new opportunities for main line running from there, McAlpine leapt at the opportunity to base her at the old GWR steam shed in Southall, not far from Paddington, in 1987. Flying Scotsman now had her own home from home. She would remain there until 2004.

The following year, 1987, was another busy year for Flying Scotsman, with charters running mainly in the Midlands and northern England. She returned to Sellafield on a series of regular trains called 'The Sellafield Sightseer' to promote the new visitor centre at the nuclear power station. However, anti-nuclear protestors ensured that, while the trains got plenty of coverage, it wasn't the sort BR wanted. (Sadly, by raising concerns about the safety of the area, the nuclear protestors inadvertently all but killed off main line steam on the beautiful Cumbrian Coast.) Flying Scotsman also ran on the south-western main line west of Basingstoke: another 'new' route for steam which had been cleared by BR. Enthusiasts would have to make the most of her, however, because McAlpine soon received an irresistible offer to take Flying Scotsman to Australia to mark the country's bicentennial. Mindful of the experience in America, there were plenty of worried people who feared that history would repeat itself.

Opposite Flying Scotsman returns from the Shildon celebrations past Benningbrough on September 2 1975 in company with GWR 'Modified Hall' 4-6-0 No. 6960 Raveningham Hall.

Below Flying Scotsman in Derby, December 1985.

AUSTRALIAN INTERLUDE

The year 1988 saw Australia celebrate its bicentennial: 200 years since Governor Phillips landed in what is now known as Botany Bay. The country was going to celebrate in style, and a group of railway enthusiasts decided to organise a 'steam spectacular' which would be held in October in Melbourne, the city where the country's first steam locomotive operated.

The Australians, like the British, take their railway heritage seriously, and each state has its own collection of historic rolling stock. The organisers of the steam spectacular wanted representatives from each state, and, to mark the connections with Britain, they also decided to try and get a British locomotive. The easiest thing to do would have been to have hired *Pendennis Castle*, which was then in Australia, from its owner Rio Tinto. The small committee organising the show decided they wanted something more iconic and famous, though. Its chairman, Melbourne postman Walter Stuchbery, approached the National Railway Museum to see if it would loan the record-holding 'A4' *Mallard*. The Museum declined as it had restored *Mallard* to working order to celebrate the fiftieth anniversary of its historic sprint down Stoke Bank, so *Mallard* was going to stay in Britain. They didn't leave Stuchbery without ideas, though; if Mallard was tied up,

they might have more success approaching Sir William McAlpine for *Flying Scotsman* instead.

McAlpine was receptive to the idea, but he did have one concern: 'I'd got the organisers to guarantee a return ticket for *Flying Scotsman* – we'd been here before!' he said. Stuchbery mortgaged his house to secure *Flying Scotsman's* return home, and McAlpine agreed to send her on another epic adventure. Hinchcliffe, who had accompanied *Flying Scotsman* to America, was also positive: 'I think it's a

Above The Puffing Billy Railway is one of the few heritage railways in Australia – but the country's enthusiasm for steam locomotives is vast. One of the diminutive train crosses the famous 1899-built Trestle Bridge, at Dandenong Ranges, Victoria, Australia.

Opposite Australian postman Walter Stuchbery came up with the idea of running *Flying Scotsman* to celebrate the nation's bicentennial in 1988. She was promoted heavily and drew crowds in their thousands.

FLYING SCOTSMAN

QANTAS **Melbourne 9th July — 6th August** P&O Containers

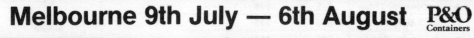

STEAMRAIL VICTORIA

is proud to support the visit of THE FLYING SCOTSMAN to Australia

STEAMRAIL VICTORIA
restores and operates
"THE VINTAGE TRAIN" ®

*Bring the Family and join us
on one of our monthly
Vintage Train excursions.*

Phone: 629 4806

*Available for Charter for your
Group Excursion, Social Club
Outing or Company Promotion.*

Phone: 397 2439

STEAMRAIL VICTORIA, *P.O. Box 61, Caulfield East. 3145*

wonderful opportunity,' he bubbled. 'And not only is the engine looking forward to it, so are all the volunteers too.'

But before she could go abroad, she had to have an air-braking system fitted in order to haul trains there as her train brakes worked on the vacuum principle and were incompatible with the air-braked coaches used in Australia. An air compressor was borrowed from the Nene Valley Railway in Cambridgeshire, and the support team, led by Kennington, worked night and day to ensure that the components most likely to fail were in tip-top condition. They even replaced the steel tyres on the driving wheels, as these were wearing thin.

Flying Scotsman departed Britain on the P&O ship *New Zealand Pacific* as deck cargo. Her loading and departure were headline news, but this was definitely 'au revoir' – McAlpine and Stuchbery had done enough to ensure that there would be no repeats of the American mishaps! On her voyage, she was doused with fresh water daily to protect her paintwork, and as she crossed the Equator was given a ceremonial splashing and a certificate to say she had crossed the Line. She was being treated more like a pampered racehorse than a steam locomotive.

Kennington, who would accompany *Flying Scotsman* throughout the tour, flew out a few days before the ship was due to arrive in Sydney. Plans to unload her in Melbourne foundered when it was discovered the crucial floating crane had been sold, so she was to be unloaded in Sydney instead.

Australian railway officials quizzed Kennington about *Flying Scotsman*. Would she, they asked, be able to climb

the 5-mile long, 1:37 Cowan Bank with a trailing load of 300 tons without assistance? What were the brake shoes made of? Were electric lights fitted? Kennington reassured them that *Flying Scotsman* would be able to cope with everything demanded of her, and with that, the officials were satisfied. She was unloaded in sight of Sydney Harbour Bridge with great care and ceremony on 16 October, and after last-minute adjustments, the Australian operating authorities certified her for main line operation. With that, Kennington and the team wasted no time in giving her a test run. With just three coaches behind her, she ran from Sydney to Port Kembla and back, a distance of 125 miles. Everything was in fine fettle, and five days after landing she was able to go to Melbourne.

The organisers planned a night-time departure to enable her to benefit from the cooler temperatures, and to spend as much time as possible at the steam spectacular. She hauled her tender, a spares van and a water tanker, and her journey wasn't expected to be noticed – but that couldn't have been more wrong. Word spread like wildfire – *Flying Scotsman* was here! Thousands upon thousands lined the tracks to see her go past: the reception was as epic as the setting.

After a settling-in period, *Flying Scotsman* began to earn her keep on passenger trains. Because there were two standard-gauge lines and one 3-feet 6-inch gauge line in parallel near Melbourne, Stuchbery and the organisers were able to arrange for three steam-hauled trains to run side-by-side. It was 'the most exciting thing' that McAlpine remembered from Australia – an absolutely spectacular sight, and it set the standard for everything that was to follow.

Large crowds were something of a problem, and it was a constant challenge to keep passengers and spectators apart. Sometimes the crew had little option but to open *Flying Scotsman's* draincocks and send a jet of steam from the cylinders in order to persuade people to get out of the way. On a trip to Albury a broken spring was noticed, quite a serious problem, but a local blacksmith came to the rescue, effecting a temporary repair which allowed *Flying Scotsman* to get back to Melbourne without further incident. *Flying Scotsman* wasn't universally popular with everyone: a hurrying motorist got hit on an unmanned level crossing. It could have been fatal, but what was beyond belief to the train crew was the fact that, after knocking off the left-hand front steps and draincock pipes, the motorist reversed the car, turned round and sped off in a cloud of smoke!

Flying Scotsman stayed in Melbourne for two months before making the 600-mile journey north back to Sydney. More than 130,000 people had paid to see her, and receipts had almost covered the transport costs. In Sydney she was welcomed, appropriately, by a pipe band and (by now to nobody's surprise) a huge crowd of over 5,000 people. During December, she was used on an intensive tour programme, the highlights of which were the times she worked with Australia's flagship 'Pacific', No. 3801. This beautiful green machine, almost the same colour as *Flying Scotsman*, and every bit as elegant, has a bullet-shaped nose and streamlined fairings, and the Australians are rightly proud of her. No. 3801 and *Flying Scotsman* were a glamorous pair, and the public adored them.

Kennington and the various volunteers, some from England, some from Australia, spent January maintaining *Flying Scotsman* to keep her in the condition to which she was accustomed. February and March saw her work a

Above *Flying Scotsman's* record-breaking non-stop run in 1988 was commemorated by a special plaque fixed under the nameplates. It remains the longest distance a steam locomotive has ever run without stopping and is unlikely to be beaten.

Opposite The reunion of two former rivals in Australia was the highlight of *Flying Scotsman's* Australian tour. Who would have put money on it happening on the other side of the world back in the 1920s when they were tested against each other? *Pendennis Castle* was every bit as popular as *Flying Scotsman*, as these crowds at East Perth terminal prove.

Below The difference in size between *Flying Scotsman* and *Pendennis Castle* is clear in this view of the two locomotives coupled together at East Perth terminal in 1988. In rebuilt 'A3' form *Flying Scotsman* was able to match the smaller locomotive for efficiency, while having far greater reserves of power in her boiler.

number of short-distance tours, though on one memorable occasion, she and No. 3801 worked the 614 miles to Brisbane. She stayed in Sydney until July, and proved a smash-hit down under, carrying thousands, and watched by many thousands more. She then returned to Melbourne briefly to prepare for an epic twenty-eight-day tour north to Alice Springs and then south again to Adelaide.

And it took some preparation: 80 tons of coal were bagged up for the trip, and three water tanks were connected first to each other, and then to *Flying Scotsman's* tender. Seven sold-out coaches carried passengers who had paid top-dollar to witness another spectacular record fall: an attempt was to be made on the non-stop steam record, which stood at 408.6 miles, recorded by 'A4' 4-6-2s hauling the 'Flying Scotsman' train in 1948. Operational preparation was critical too. The 422 miles between Parkes and Broken Hill was single-track, and trains could only pass at short sections of double-track called loops. Four trains had to be crossed and water had to be pumped from the tank wagons to the tender. In the coach behind the tanks waited a crew member with a petrol-driven water pump. On the order, he would start the pump, and some of the 26,000 gallons of water would go into *Flying Scotsman's* tender.

The run on 8 August 1989 was truly heroic. Even though there were problems with two of the critical token exchanges, without which *Flying Scotsman* would not have been permitted on to sections of single track, and even though a lorry crossed the line just a few feet in front of the train 80 miles short of the destination, *Flying Scotsman* performed like the thoroughbred she was. After 9 hours and 25 minutes, *Flying Scotsman* arrived at Broken Hill, having consumed just 16,000 gallons of her 25,000-gallon water supply. 'We could have gone much, much further!'

Opposite Australia's equivalent of *Flying Scotsman* is the beautiful streamlined 'Pacific' No. 3801. She draws an admiring crowd on a trial run on 19 January 1943.

Below In a rare moment of peace, *Flying Scotsman* stands in the evening sunlight at East Perth terminal, 1988.

beamed a delighted McAlpine, who was on the train at the time.

The final stage of the journey to Alice Springs was memorable for different reasons. The old narrow-gauge line had just been replaced by standard-gauge track, and *Flying Scotsman* would be the first steam locomotive to traverse it: in fact, she would be the first steam locomotive in Alice Springs for years. The 775-mile line was long enough for a diesel locomotive to be attached to the train in case *Flying Scotsman* failed, but that was never likely with Kennington on the shovel, and the able hand of former Top Shed 'Pacific' driver David Rollins on the regulator.

This wasn't a non-stop run, and efforts were made to stop en route to give as many people as possible the chance to see the locomotive. As a result the journey took 30 hours in total, but arrival in Alice Springs was worth the wait. McAlpine, who was on the footplate, was overwhelmed by what he saw: 'When we went there, they closed schools, and people were lining the track for miles. I think the whole town must have turned out!' Of all the welcomes accorded *Flying Scotsman* during her stay in Australia, this was the most spectacular. The local Aboriginal people staged a ceremony too, welcoming *Flying Scotsman* formally to their land: it was a unique recognition of her personality and character.

She returned from Alice Springs to Adelaide, but, while the original plan had been to go to Sydney for her journey home, it was now decided she should go to Perth instead. Crossing the world's longest straight bit of railway, 297 miles of arrow-straight track on the Nullarbor Plain, she took five days. During that time, problems with the air compressor meant that a diesel locomotive was needed to assist braking, and the hard water had fractured piston rings in the right-hand cylinder and damaged the valve head, leading to some cautious running.

It was a long, tiring journey, but Western Australia rolled out the red carpet for *Flying Scotsman*, the public's appetite for this iconic locomotive undimmed by time. Here, something truly amazing had been arranged – something

that you'd have got incredible odds from the bookmaker you'd placed a bet even five years before. *Flying Scotsm*⌐ came smokebox-to-smokebox with her old rival and form⌐ stablemate *Pendennis Castle*. 'That was amazing,' recalls McAlpine, 'because I actually had a painting of the two o⌐ them together at Carnforth commissioned, because I ne⌐ thought I would see them together again. Off *Pendennis* went, and in Australia they met buffer to buffer!' It was a⌐ emotional reunion, and for a few blissful weeks, the pair worked special trains, occasionally double-heading. It was a fitting climax to a tour that had succeeded beyond anyone's expectations.

It couldn't last forever, and after spending a short time in Sydney, where she spent a short time running, gaining

minutes on the 24-minute schedule on the notorious
wan Bank (one of the steepest railway gradients in
ustralia), *Flying Scotsman* was loaded on the French cargo
ip *La Perouse*, heading on the easterly route via Cape
orn to to Tilbury. In the process, she became the first
comotive to circumnavigate the globe.

For all involved, the visit to Australia had been a massive
ccess. Stuchbery's dream of seeing *Flying Scotsman*
Melbourne had come true, and thousands (probably
ndreds of thousands) of people who might never have
eamed of seeing her in the flesh got their chance. She
d run something like 28,000 miles without a critical
ilure, and she had looked magnificent throughout. From
e ecstatic receptions she received, to the unbelievable

non-stop run, it had been a fantastic year, and one which
will live long in the memories of everyone involved.

Above Having set records in the 1920s and 1930s, amazingly *Flying
Scotsman* managed another in 1989, running 422 miles non-stop
between Parkes and Broken Hill. It remains the longest non-stop
distance ever covered by a steam locomotive.

RETURN

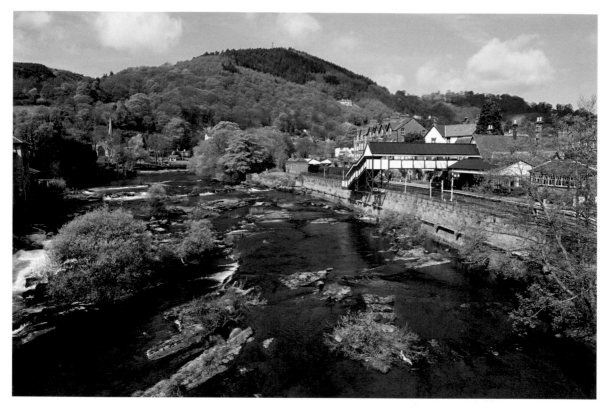

flying Scotsman landed safely back in Britain just before Christmas 1989. Her tour to Australia had been a huge success, and the locomotive was headline news again. On arrival at Southall, engineer Roland Kennington immediately gave her a thorough inspection, but to his delight, found she needed relatively little work to make her fit for service.

Her first run back in Britain was on a special train called 'The FSS Executive', which ran from Didcot to Banbury. The managing director of British Rail's (BR) InterCity sector, Dr John Prideaux, unveiled a plaque below her nameplates to commemorate the epic non-stop run between Parkes and Broken Hill. Thankfully for the enthusiasts, there was no further talk of foreign adventures!

Flying Scotsman next found herself temporarily based at Crewe to work trains on the delightful North Wales Coast line to Holyhead. Though it was unfamiliar territory, she performed impeccably, winning new admirers in the Principality she had first visited in 1963. However, on one of the trains, disaster struck when a passenger leaning out of a door window struck his head on the wall of Penmaenbach

Above The Llangollen Railway in Wales was one of the 'second generation' of heritage railways and its headquarters station perches delicately next to the River Dee. It was on this railway that Flying Scotsman suffered damage that effectively finished her career under the ownership of Sir William McAlpine.

Opposite Flying Scotsman's first run in Britain was the 'FSS Executive' railtour, and despite her hard work in Australia, she needed little work to return her to traffic.

Following pages In response to enthusiasts' pleas, McAlpine repainted Flying Scotsman in the last in-service livery of British Railways, complete with German-style smoke deflectors. This is what the locomotive looked like when Alan Pegler acquired her in 1963.

Tunnel and died. Many enthusiasts travelling on rail tours appreciated the drop-down windows on the doors (through which the doors were opened from the inside), as they could lean out and see the locomotive hauling the train. At the time of the accident there was a great deal of soul-searching, but reluctantly, the decision was taken to fit bars to the windows to prevent a repeat of the tragedy.

In September 1990, to mark the twenty-fifth anniversary of the popular Severn Valley Railway in Shropshire, *Flying Scotsman* made a rare visit to a preserved line, and the heritage railway was rewarded with full trains and linesides packed with people taking pictures. 'If you charged £1 for every picture taken,' says a wistful McAlpine, 'you could overhaul her every year!'

Flying Scotsman's condition was still reasonable, but she was rapidly approaching the end of her seven-year main line boiler certificate. McAlpine, who had long recognised that *Flying Scotsman* was most profitable visiting heritage railways, decided that, rather than undergo another expensive seven-year overhaul, she should go on tour to such railways around the country until her boiler certificate ran out in a couple of years' time.

This was something that hadn't been possible when McAlpine repatriated *Flying Scotsman* in the 1970s. Then there were just a handful of heritage railways, and few were long enough, or had good enough facilities, to handle an engine of her size. The track on many was lightly laid and would have taken a battering too. But in the intervening twenty years, the heritage railway movement had blossomed, and there were now three lines longer than 15 miles, and a good few approaching 10 miles: long enough for *Flying Scotsman* to stretch her legs.

More crucially, passenger numbers had boomed too. A combination of great marketing, public nostalgia and the influence of Thomas the Tank Engine on the little ones meant that heritage railways were now regarded as key tourist attractions in almost every area they served. Engineering capabilities had also improved in leaps and bounds. Whereas replacing the boiler tubes of a locomotive in the 1970s would have seemed a major task, creative and brilliant engineers had devised ways of keeping the giants of steam running safely for longer than anyone had anticipated. The time was right for *Flying Scotsman* to rejoin this movement.

Heritage railways around the country submitted bids to run *Flying Scotsman*, and she immediately proved a smash hit. When she visited the Birmingham Railway Museum in Tyseley, she was used on 'driver experience' duties, where, for a fee, members of the public could have the opportunity to drive and fire this priceless icon, under

close supervision, of course. She then visited the Great Central Railway at Loughborough, and the East Lancashire Railway at Bury before heading back into Wales to visit the Llangollen Railway.

The Llangollen Railway is among the prettiest in Britain, and at 6 miles had long offered a reasonable opportunity for *Flying Scotsman* to stretch her legs. A wide-ranging variety of duties was planned, from ordinary passenger trains, to driver experience courses, to dining trains, all in a bid to give as many people as possible as many ways to experience *Flying Scotsman* as possible. The aim was to raise money for much-needed track and bridge improvements, and *Flying Scotsman* offered a really good way of raising funds.

However, on arrival at Llangollen in March 1993, it became apparent that *Flying Scotsman* was not in good enough health to do any running at all. While she was with the Great Central Railway, a leak from one of the flue tubes in the boiler had been noticed. It started off as a minor leak from the boiler into the tubes the fire passed through, and in all probability sealed up as soon as the boiler got hot and expanded slightly. But, as ever is the case with these things, the problem gradually got worse. By the time *Flying Scotsman* had reached Bury, the tubes required attention every morning before she started in service, and by Llangollen the leak was described, memorably, as being like a waterfall. There was no way she could operate safely. The Llangollen Railway made the best of a bad job by offering

footplate visits at £1 a time, so *Flying Scotsman's* visit wasn't entirely in vain.

There was little point in spending a huge amount of money on *Flying Scotsman's* boiler, but salvation was at hand when the West Midlands engineering firm of FKI Babcock Robey agreed to retube the boiler at no charge: at their Oldbury worksite wanted the world to know about the quality of its workmanship and the generosity of the company. For the first time since 19 February 1963, she was to appear in public in her last front-line livery, the Brunswick green of British Railways, after her volunteers asked McAlpine for permission. Conscious of the immense effort and commitment they had given the locomotive, he readily agreed. She was fitted with a double chimney,

given smoke-deflecting plates at the side of the smokebox, and renumbered to 60103. She couldn't have looked more different from the apple-green colour she had by now carried for most of her life if she'd wanted to.

The year 1993 was a momentous one. After thirty years of outright ownership, McAlpine went into partnership with the music mogul and rail enthusiast Pete Waterman. McAlpine had bought the Pullman train from the Steam Locomotive Owners' Association (SLOA) after the boss of InterCity's special trains unit, David Ward, suggested that he bought his own set of carriages to keep them running. It was sound advice because, with privatisation of the railways on the horizon, there was no guarantee these increasingly venerable coaches would receive the same care and attention that InterCity lavished on them. But to McAlpine's horror – and in all likelihood to Ward's surprise – asbestos was found in some of the coaches during overhaul. As the material was now banned, specialist contractors had to be found to remove it safely.

Waterman, meanwhile, had been busy acquiring a number of diesel and steam locomotives in anticipation of privatisation. Waterman wanted to run the first train in privatisation, and had spent a fortune overhauling a heritage diesel to demanding standards in a bid to break the preserved diesel ban that BR had imposed when enthusiasts started to buy surplus locomotives.

By the early 1990s, BR was among the most efficient state-owned railways in the world. It had finally found the holy grail of organisation which had proved so elusive since 1923 – rather than organising things on a regional basis, the railway was managed based on the type of traffic. This meant that commuter trains around London were in one part of the organisation, and freight in another; Scotland's services were in a separate company; long-distance express services were run by InterCity (a massive success story in its own right); and local and regional services everywhere else were operated by the BR division. Even after all the privatisations of the 1980s, Margaret Thatcher found herself acknowledging that BR was working well, and that to privatise it would be like selling the family silver.

However, John Major's government, which succeeded Thatcher's, disagreed. The railway would be sold and split up so comprehensively that renationalisation would be difficult if not impossible. The plan was to have one

left Only one other locomotive can claim to have the same level of fame as *Flying Scotsman* – the fictional character Thomas the Tank Engine. Over the years replicas of the blue engine have drawn similar crowds to No. 4472 at heritage railways, albeit with a much younger audience. This is an event at Llangollen on the Llangollen Railway.

company owning the tracks, which would be floated on the stock market. The rail freight companies were to be sold off in their entirety too, but passenger trains were to be run on a franchised basis. Traffic was split up first by type, and then by region, so that there were more than twenty companies operating passenger trains. Furthermore – and this was why Waterman wanted to run trains – any company that wanted to do so could (providing it met certain financial and safety criteria) run trains on the network: something known as 'open access'. This meant Waterman could run charter trains in his own right without depending on another company to provide locomotives, carriages and staff. Privatisation was too tempting for him to resist.

Waterman had been an apprentice in the 1960s at the former Great Western Railway (GWR) locomotive works in Stafford Road, Wolverhampton, before embarking on a highly successful career in showbiz that included launching the careers of Kylie Minogue and Jason Donovan, among others. He had seen the reaction of visitors to the East Lancashire Railway, rang McAlpine, and after a meeting in May 1993 the pair agreed to go into partnership.

Though McAlpine acknowledges that sharing the financial burden of running *Flying Scotsman* was part of his motivation, he was also concerned about the future. 'I am not immortal, and if I had died without making plans, *Flying Scotsman* could possibly have ended up in a situation that would not have been in her best interests,' he said at the time. 'Now, Pete is a little younger than I, and I now feel that the locomotive's future is secure.' The sentiment is typical of the man – while retaining his sound business sense, he was also looking ahead, and felt strongly that *Flying Scotsman* should stay running rather than being a stuffed-and-mounted exhibit at a museum.

Released to traffic in 1993 in the guise of her final, most powerful form, *Flying Scotsman* went back on tour of the preserved lines. First was the Dartmouth Steam Railway which she had visited thirty years before, then to the Gloucestershire and Warwickshire Railway, the Nene Valley Railway in Peterborough, and the Swanage and Severn Valley Railways, before visiting the Birmingham Railway Museum again. Finally, in the spring of 1995, in the last year of her boiler certificate, she reached the Llangollen Railway, where it was hoped she would repay her debt of honour to the dedicated volunteers there.

She came agonisingly close to doing so, but then suffered what engineers call an 'all-wheels' derailment at low speed. While one set of wheels can usually be jacked back on to the rails, this was rather trickier to recover, and specialist lifting gear had to be called out from Crewe. Once on the rails, a crack in the firebox soon became apparent. This was worse than a leaking tube, and the insurance inspector sent to see if the boiler was safe soon gave McAlpine and Waterman his verdict: 'If it was a horse, I'd have it shot,' he said.

Below Music mogul Pete Waterman started his working life on the railways and has been a lifelong enthusiast. As privatisation began in the mid-1990s he partnered with McAlpine with a view to running charters with *Flying Scotsman* and his own fleet on parts of the main line that had not seen steam locomotives since the 1960s.

There was no option: *Flying Scotsman* had to come back to Southall for overhaul, but McAlpine and Waterman could spare neither the time nor the money to give *Flying Scotsman* top priority, because their partnership business was becoming increasingly time-consuming as the complexities of privatisation became all too apparent. Funds became tight, and *Flying Scotsman* was mortgaged to secure the future of their joint venture.

By March 1996 Waterman revealed to the press that he was 'totally fed up' with the privatisation process. His ambitions to make money from the privatised railway were thwarted, and he offered his surplus locomotives for sale. The fact that it took longer than expected to remove the

asbestos from the former SLOA Pullman coaches McAlpine had acquired also deprived the partnership of a potentially lucrative revenue stream for a whole season. Too much happened in too short a time, and Waterman decided to curtail his active involvement in the rail industry, though his Waterman Railways company eventually refocused on engineering, rebranded itself as LNWR, and operated from Crewe. The partnership between Waterman and McAlpine never went bust, despite popular myth and, while *Flying Scotsman* was unlikely to steam in the near future, at least she was safe.

Above The next owner of *Flying Scotsman*, Tony Marchington, stands on the running plate of the locomotive during her extensive overhaul at Southall, London.

In 1996, *Flying Scotsman* faced an uncertain operational future. Neither Pete Waterman or William McAlpine were keen to spend yet more money on an expensive overhaul and, now out of traffic and with no revenue stream, it looked like it was going to be a while before she would steam again. Waterman and McAlpine were busy trying to make a success of the former British Rail (BR) special trains unit, which was sold at privatisation: as McAlpine says, *Flying Scotsman* had to take a back seat. In an interview, Waterman casually mentioned that *Flying Scotsman* was worth £1.3 million. He didn't say he and McAlpine wanted to sell her: they didn't – but that was the inference many drew. It didn't take long for a buyer to make an approach.

The man in question was a successful businessman, long-time steam enthusiast and self-confessed traction engine 'nut', Dr Tony Marchington. Marchington had just floated his biotechnology company Oxford Molecular, and, by all accounts, had £5 million burning a hole in his pocket. Marchington had a lifelong passion for steam which inexorably drew him towards *Flying Scotsman*. He was passionate about the locomotive and wanted to see it run on the main line.

Marchington wasted no time in getting in touch with McAlpine. He wanted to spend £1.3 million on the locomotive, and another £300,000 or so overhauling her for main line operation. So Marchington acquired *Flying Scotsman* from McAlpine and Waterman and started to formulate his plans to make her pay. This wasn't a purchase made on a whim. Marchington had formulated a daring, but apparently sensible business plan, which would see *Flying*

Scotsman and another locomotive he acquired – 'A4' No. 60019 *Bittern* – hauling a series of £250-per-head dining trains from the London area.

Marchington had budgeted an overhaul cost of around £300,000: in line with that of other similar sized engines that had needed similar work at the time. Nobody could have expected the ferocious cost of bringing *Flying Scotsman* back to life. Over the first three years of ownership Marchington spent a gigantic £750,000 rebuilding the engine to operational standards. Many suggested *Flying Scotsman* was jinxed and had some kind of curse because it caused so much trouble for Alan Pegler in America, and the spiralling cost of the 1996–99 overhaul did nothing to dissuade those views. During the overhaul, Marchington wasn't able to earn a penny back as the locomotive was stripped down to her component parts for the rebuild, and eventually further finance had to be sought to continue with the project. He went to the banks: a reasonable short-term decision given the credibility of his business case. The overhaul of *Flying Scotsman* was managed by Roland Kennington with the locomotive's frames and tender remaining at Southall, West London, for volunteer overhaul,

whilst the boiler was sent to Chatham Steam Restorations for a thorough check-over and repair.

It may have cost a fortune, but when *Flying Scotsman* was unveiled to the public on 28 May 1999 few doubted it was money well spent. It was the first time Marchington had seen *Flying Scotsman* complete and in steam since he bought her three years earlier.

Below *Flying Scotsman's* boiler is painted grey, a sign that the overhaul is nearing completion as a volunteer runs an oily rag over a coupling rod at Southall.

Two months after her public debut, *Flying Scotsman* was back on home turf, standing at London King's Cross station waiting to haul her first main line special since the early 1990s. This train, the first under Marchington's ownership, was a sell-out, £350-per-head return trip to York, and it was just the start of what appeared to be a promising time for *Flying Scotsman* and Dr Marchington's business Oxford Molecular.

The East Coast Main Line was where Marchington wanted to run his premium dining trains. They would capture the London market and offer real steam haulage by *Flying Scotsman* on her original route: another part of his business plan that made perfect sense commercially, and for those with a sense of history. Initially, the main line turns loaded

well, and it looked like Marchington's plan was going to justify the faith he'd shown in funding *Flying Scotsman's* overhaul. But in October 2000, *Flying Scotsman's* world fell apart as Britain's entire railway network went into meltdown following a derailment caused by a broken rail.

Unable to confirm that similar rails all around the country were safe, draconian speed restrictions of 20mph were imposed across the network. Ordinary service trains took hours longer than before to reach their destinations, and for *Flying Scotsman* and other steam locomotives, there was no way they could continue operating on the main line. At a stroke, much of *Flying Scotsman's* cash flow dried up. Marchington reluctantly decided to sell the Pullman coaches and *Bittern* in order to try and keep

allowed Marchington to continue his involvement with the locomotive while other people were paid to manage the day-to-day business. Few other locomotives have attracted such lucrative work, and during 2002 *Flying Scotsman* was booked to haul sixty-eight trains for VSOE, a very respectable amount of work. However, Tony Marchington wasn't only serious about owning *Flying Scotsman*, but also about his other passion for traction engines. This division of his passion, which had proved so crucial in getting *Flying Scotsman* running so well would ultimately, but unintentionally, place a national icon in jeopardy.

Left Southall Motive Power Depot was originally a Great Western Railway facility but since becoming a preservation base has developed the ability to take on crucial running repairs and much restoration of steam locomotives. Marchington uprated *Flying Scotsman* to cope with the heavier work he planned for her – with mixed results.

Below The October 2000 derailment at Hatfield threw the rail network into chaos over concerns about the state of the track. With many journeys extended by hours in the weeks afterwards steam was effectively banned from the main line for a while – with disastrous effects on Marchington's business plan.

alive the possibility that *Flying Scotsman* could continue running.

With little other revenue, a lucrative contract was needed to keep *Flying Scotsman* in service, and that was achieved in 2001 when Marchington landed a five-year deal to haul around fifty luxury dining trains per year for the British part of the Venice-Simplon Orient Express company (VSOE). It was a marvellous deal for both parties. That contract became *Flying Scotsman's* main source of income as the engine was given a monopoly for the luxury trains that would see her paid very well for each job. There was a good chance the locomotive could earn her keep.

In 2001 Marchington transferred ownership to Flying Scotsman Plc. There was nothing strange about this as it

The real battles began when Dr Marchington chose to send *Flying Scotsman* to the Derbyshire Steam Fair in the Peak District in June 2002 to stand on a 100-foot length of track. But rather than doing this on a day when the engine wasn't booked for main line duties with VSOE, he decided to take her away from the £5,000-per-day VSOE work and send it to the rally instead – for free. This didn't just cause trouble with her main contractor VSOE, but also within the volunteer engineering team which kept the engine running. In fact, so strong was the tension that the volunteer team refused to accompany *Flying Scotsman* to the rally.

Whilst VSOE was upbeat about the opportunity to operate different prestigious locomotives at the head of its luxury dining trains as a positive move for its passengers, who would then be guaranteed steam haulage, it was less than satisfied that *Flying Scotsman* might not be available again on 12 June.

A share issue by Flying Scotsman Plc to raise funds captured the imagination of the media and it received a great boost in publicity. Not all was as it appeared in the press, as while it appeared that buyers were purchasing shares in *Flying Scotsman* they were actually buying shares in the company – a very different beast. Success would prove elusive. The first signs that all was not well came in January 2002 when the deadline for shares sales came and went without the shares selling out. The deadline was extended. Still the shares issue didn't perform as expected. In total £850,000 worth of shares were sold – less than half of the target of £2.2 million shares.

For three years Flying Scotsman Plc traded a loss. In 2001 it lost £360,000 and a year later a loss of £555,929. Marchington had already placed himself in the firing line once when he transferred ownership of *Flying Scotsman* to Flying Scotsman Plc while he retained the original

and valuable nameplates, but in 2002 the revelation hit the streets that he was planning to sell both original nameplates from *Flying Scotsman*. Marchington's decision caused uproar in the steam movement.

Britain's biggest railwayana auction house, Sheffield Railwayana, was offered the opportunity to sell the nameplates for £50,000 each, but declined. Marchington continued to try and sell these most famous of nameplates elsewhere.

Later in 2002, at an auction in Derbyshire held by Smith Hodgkinson, the nameplates were listed again. Despite a bid of £55,000 the nameplates weren't sold, but many items from Dr Marchington's private traction engine collection did sell, raising £700,000. By now Marchington was apparently running out of cash.

Things were not going well on the VSOE deal. The company that had provided *Flying Scotsman* with such a substantial income gave the contract to haul its luxury train in the north of England, the 'Northern Belle', to the Princess Royal Class Locomotive Trust, which operates Stanier 'Duchess' No. 6233 *Duchess of Sutherland*. This was a big problem for the Plc, as the estimated loss in earnings of £65,000 per year represented a fifth of the annual income for the locomotive. *Flying Scotsman's* duties on VSOE's trains from London were reduced by seven to just thirty-two trains for 2003.

At the end of 2002 and start of 2003, *Flying Scotsman* received more bad news when her intermediate overhaul overran by sixteen weeks. Just seven were allocated for the 'Pacific' to be out of traffic, the total was twenty-three. It was routine but challenging maintenance: unfortunately *Flying Scotsman* and her team simply fell victim to unexpected glitches that sometimes accompany overhauls. It was bad luck, but it couldn't have come at a much worse time.

If everything had gone according to plan *Flying Scotsman* would have been back out on the main line at the head of a VSOE special from London on 15 February. With the showstopping engine not available VSOE turned, once again, to *Union of South Africa*. With the overhaul overrunning by so long, *Union of South Africa* was called upon twice more before *Flying Scotsman* was able to return to the main line. Now, though, the Plc was saddled with an undisclosed bill for its overhaul and the loss of a substantial portion of the year's earnings from its lucrative contract.

By now VSOE must have felt that it couldn't risk relying on *Flying Scotsman* alone because it decided to take a powerful stance with Flying Scotsman Plc. It took away the exclusive rights for *Flying Scotsman* to haul the London-based trains. It was yet another nail in the coffin for the Plc, as the work allocated initially to *Flying Scotsman* would have amounted to fifty trains – or in round figures – approximately £250,000.

Opposite above The opulence of the British Venice-Simplon Orient Express is clear. Here passengers are greeted by uniformed staff at carriage doors …

Opposite below … and then transported into a world removed from the modern day railway, with fine dining and luxurious accommodation as standard.

Above *Flying Scotsman* poses outside her Doncaster Works birthplace at the 2003 open day. A year later she would finally be owned by the general public.

A month after *Flying Scotsman* finally returned to the rails, in June 2003, Marchington resigned from Flying Scotsman Plc, seven years after spending £1.3 million to buy the world's most famous and highly-regarded railway locomotive ever built. Marchington had funded a comprehensive and beautifully completed overhaul, and he had fought tooth and nail to keep her on the main line. It was the right time to step out of the limelight.

Marchington had the largest single shareholding in Flying Scotsman Plc, but not the overall majority. When he quit the Plc *Flying Scotsman* had ripped every pound from his pocket to keep her in running order, and possibly more. Now, the locomotive continued her weekly operations solely under the jurisdiction of the Plc, with no input whatsoever from the man who bought her in 1996. By now the Plc was solely reliant on the VSOE contract to bring in any cash at all.

Ironically, given all the turmoil around her, a happy moment in 2003 for the 'Pacific' was her appearance at the fabulous Doncaster Works 150th anniversary event held in July that year. For the event *Flying Scotsman* received a brand new coat of London and North Eastern Railway (LNER) apple-green paint paid for by Wabtec, Doncaster Works' owner, and was back in the place where she was built in 1923. Better still, the event brought together what will be remembered as the greatest preservation gathering of ex-LNER locomotives of all shapes and sizes, from the magnificent Stirling 'Single' to the world's fastest steam locomotive, Gresley's sublime 'A4' No. 4468 *Mallard*. The event attracted 31,000 visitors and *Flying Scotsman* was the number-one attraction.

The triumph of the event soon paled into insignificance as two months later much more serious issues were on the table. Marchington declared himself bankrupt after shares in Oxford Molecular plummeted on the stock market and the company failed. The owner had no money, the Plc which had custody of the locomotive had no money, and there was none set aside for the next £300,000–500,000 overhaul. Storm clouds were forming over *Flying Scotsman*.

This was *Flying Scotsman's* darkest hour since being stranded in the United States in the 1970s. The locomotive had led a safe life in preservation since 1973, but now her future was bleak. *Flying Scotsman* continued to run on the main line through 2003, but with debts continuing to rise. The loan taken out by Marchington and secured against the locomotive was transferred to the Plc with the engine in 2001, and in 2003 the interest alone is believed to have amounted to over £200,000. Money troubles didn't end there. Directors' salaries were being paid from Flying Scotsman earnings and the losses were beginning to snowball. In 2002 the Plc made a loss of £474,619 and earned just £238,102.

Grave news came that autumn when it was revealed that Flying Scotsman Plc would almost certainly run out of money in nine months' time at the annual general meeting on 22 October. Auctioneers had been lined up to sell the locomotive if repayments to the £1.5 million loan secured against it were not paid.

Fears rose that the locomotive might be sold abroad. Now there were no illusions: only someone very wealthy could afford to run such a machine and there was also the possibility that she might be placed on static display, never to turn a wheel again. The inevitable happened and Flying Scotsman was put on the market for sale to the highest bidder. The reserve was £2 million.

Flying Scotsman has always sparked debate and interest, but never more so than when she came on the market following the collapse of Flying Scotsman Plc in early 2004. One car auctioneer connected with the sale talked of the engine achieving an £8 million sale price – more than eight times the price expected for a similar sized locomotive, and a figure that would build at least two new steam locomotives based on 'new-build' Peppercorn 'A1' No. 60163 Tornado's construction cost of around £3m.

As Flying Scotsman Plc's financial situation worsened fears for the locomotive's future grew. First came the revelation that the engine was being touted for sale by classic car dealer Malcolm Elder. The car dealer had overseas contacts, and very quickly the possibility of Flying Scotsman being sold abroad became a real concern. Initially the possibility of an auction to sell No. 4472 was denied by Flying Scotsman Plc Chairman Peter Shea, but the valuations had already been made ranging from a few hundred thousand pounds to £8 million. In February 2004 debt agency GVA Grimley made Flying Scotsman officially available for sale on behalf of Flying Scotsman Plc via a sealed-bid auction. Until the new owner was revealed in April, no one could know who the new owner of this most famous steam locomotive would be.

Barclays wanted to recoup the £1.2 million overdraft that the Plc had racked up, and even though some commentators believed the 'Pacific' was really, in physical terms, worth around £500,000–750,000, the final sale price was still estimated at between £1 and £2 million. A quick sale was wanted and even though the sale was only announced in February, the deadline was just six weeks away on 2 April.

Within days of her sale being announced the whole of the UK and much of the western world would hear of her plight. Her status as a British icon took the story into the daily papers, and it is known to have appeared in at least one American newspaper, The New York Times, around the time of the sale.

Fears of a sale abroad subsided a little as in theory, export law potentially prevented Flying Scotsman leaving the country, but only temporarily. If an overseas bidder was successful in securing Flying Scotsman the locomotive might not be allowed to leave the country straight away. Six months would be allowed for a UK counter-bid to be prepared. Time was short, and very quickly bidders started to marshal support.

Several private buyers made their interest in the locomotive clear to the auctioneers, with former National Railway Museum (NRM) Head Andrew Dow and private businessman Jeremy Hosking both considering the purchase. Dow wished to set up a trust to look after the future of Flying Scotsman and even went as far as to begin negotiations with the Heritage Lottery Fund and plan for a public appeal. At the time Dow said: 'I think it is clear by now that Scotsman can never have a future in private hands. The situation has clearly got to change.'

On the other hand, Hosking was reported to be weighing up his options over Flying Scotsman. He already had a substantial collection of locomotives but even Hosking wasn't sure whether Flying Scotsman should remain in private hands. Talking to Steam Railway magazine in March 2004 he said: 'I genuinely haven't decided if I'm going to bid.

'I'm very interested to know what the railway community thinks about the locomotive being owned by the NRM. Most of us are concerned about Flying Scotsman and want what is best for it. With the NRM determined to bid and getting the support of the Heritage Lottery Fund, it makes the whole question of whether to bid a complicated issue.'

That sentiment was echoed throughout the preservation movement and the top of the chain, the NRM also began to take interest in Flying Scotsman's sale. There was a public desire calling for this famous machine to become part of the NRM collection. Even with its presence in the steam preservation movement, the NRM would never have been handed Flying Scotsman on a plate. It would have to pay for her, just like any other bidder, and there came the biggest problem.

The NRM, while being a tremendous organisation, wouldn't have the spare cash to part with the minimum £1.5 million to be in with a chance of winning a sealed bid for Flying Scotsman. But what it did have was a huge amount of support from railway enthusiasts and most importantly the general public. When the sale was announced, the then NRM Head Andrew Scott was in Japan with former Head of Collections Helen Ashby, attending a conference on railway conservation and for visits to the NRM's two partner museums during their stay. Scott was alerted to the news by email and he was able to respond quickly: 'We knew we would have to work quite hard to make a workable bid, and we contacted York to let them know that we would be going ahead,' he said.

Scott wasn't surprised that the situation had come to a head: 'I think we'd not been convinced that Flying Scotsman Plc's business plan was sustainable for some time. I know I wasn't the only one who wondered whether it was deliverable. There was a definite feeling that things would come to a head.'

In anticipation of this situation, Scott and the NRM had had quiet talks with the National Heritage Memorial Fund (NHMF) to sound them out about the likelihood of winning funds, should a rescue bid for *Flying Scotsman* be necessary. The fund gave them a clear steer in the affirmative.

Anyone who wanted to secure this most famous of steam locomotives had to act quickly, but the NRM also had to think carefully about how the locomotive would fit in with the collection. On his return to York, Scott began discussions about the appropriateness of *Flying Scotsman* joining the National Collection. Many had mourned the fact that No. 4472 wasn't selected for the National Collection by the British Transport Commission back in 1963 when she was withdrawn, but they were thankful that Alan Pegler had stepped in to save the day. Now it was someone else's turn. Scott's mind was clear: 'Nobody could argue that *Flying Scotsman* doesn't deserve a place in the museum on a

Opposite A metal workshop at Doncaster Works, South Yorkshire, c. 1916. Facilities like these made overhaul of locomotives and carriages relatively straightforward but since their decline heritage railways have had to develop their own capabilities.

Below Sir Richard Branson was quick to support the Save Our Scotsman campaign, offering to match the general public's donations. His generosity and that of thousands of enthusiasts of all ages – plus government grants – secured the locomotive's future.

OVERHAULING A STEAM LOCOMOTIVE

For steam locomotives the world has changed massively since BR steam came to an end in 1968. Back in the 1950s new components were available off the shelf at major works and repair was often by replacement. Things are very different today: few if any parts are available off the shelf meaning that they have to be repaired, fabricated or made from new. Advances in repair techniques have made it possible to repair or replace just about every single component. The specialist engineering involved in repairing a locomotive boiler comes at a price, and it has to be done right first time as the boiler and the running gear are highly-specialised and safety-critical pieces of precision engineering. With these essentially hand-built machines until engineers begin stripping out the internal components and analysing the metal no one really knows what repairs will be necessary. Steam locomotives aren't easy machines to work on – and neither are they cheap to overhaul. This combination of high cost and – to an extent – unknown condition is the main reason why steam locomotive overhauls sometimes overrun their budgets, though seldom to the extent of *Flying Scotsman's* latest overhaul.

historical basis: the story of *Flying Scotsman* is the story of the railways.'

Although the NRM was now actively planning a rescue bid, it came as a surprise to many that *Flying Scotsman* wasn't already owned by it. The NRM had an opportunity with a public appeal, and that is just what it did with only six weeks to raise the massive target of more than £1.5 million to be in with a chance of saving *Flying Scotsman* for the nation. Simultaneously the people of Britain had a once in a lifetime chance to give *Flying Scotsman* the home that its iconic status deserved in the National Collection.

The NRM had to prepare its bid. A final decision from the NHMF was expected in late March, but that still left a major shortfall, as in order to secure potentially 90 per cent of the funding from the NHMF the NRM had to raise the remaining 10 per cent. The NRM launched the Save Our Scotsman campaign. The effect was massive. The appeal itself was launched in a blaze of glory in York in co-operation with the LNER's train operator successor, Great North Eastern Railway. The result was astonishing – a sustained burst of publicity highlighting the engine's situation, and warning that it could be sold abroad. It struck

Above The National Railway Museum's success in acquiring *Flying Scotsman* was confirmed on 5 April 2004. On that day she was moved out of her shed at Southall in preparation for exhibition at the York Railfest.

a chord with the public, whose heartstrings had been pulled by the thought of losing *Flying Scotsman*.

Even though initial publicity had been favourable, there was no guarantee that a public appeal would be successful. The entrepreneur Richard Branson offered a lifeline by offering to match pound for pound the public's donations. His support came at a crucial time. His Virgin company ran the West Coast Main Line's long-distance trains (and now has a stake in the Virgin Trains East Coast operation) and his high public profile guaranteed more publicity. His motivation to support the campaign had little to do with his train companies: 'The big chequebooks of American museums have taken too many wonderful things away from Britain, and that's why we decided to intervene and keep it here,' he said.

Branson's generosity was boosted by good news from the NHMF, which granted £1.8 million towards the engine's purchase, but more support was still needed. The appeal touched everyone from every background and even those who had no recollection of it in service. It's just such a national treasure.

A press call at *Flying Scotsman's* Southall base to highlight the locomotive's situation also proved to be a real turning point as it gave the NRM access to national and international media, who despite their protestations to the contrary, generally prefer to cover stories close to their bases in the capital. That placed the appeal on the national agenda which in turn lifted the profile to a national and international appeal.

With Branson's generous offer to match the public's donations, money was coming in fast through the public appeal. But that wasn't all: Yorkshire Forward, the regional development agency, came forward with a grant for around £500,000. The money was starting to come together.

The public response to the NRM's campaign really was quite exceptional. People of all ages donated their change whilst a few individuals with the finance and specific interest in seeing *Flying Scotsman* saved for the nation would dig deep into their pockets and add sizeable sums to the fund themselves.

In less than a month the appeal drew 6,000 individual donations amounting to £365,000, ranging from £1 to £50,000. Andrew Scott almost found it overwhelming: 'It was the most amazing thing seeing this avalanche of paper come in every morning.' The Friends of the National Railway Museum also joined in, pledging £25,000 to the campaign. Wherever you were in the country you couldn't fail to hear about the museum's appeal, even though it only had six short weeks to come up with the massive £2 million asking price.

As the deadline loomed, there was still uncertainty about whether the funds raised by the NRM would be enough. At one stage there the auctioneers stated that there could be around fifteen serious bidders with an interest in the apple-green icon, though only the NRM had made its intentions publicly known.

As the deadline of 2 April 2004 approached tension became almost palpable in York. The NRM's brilliant emotive, sustained and assertive campaign had secured funding of £3 million for the locomotive, though it was always intended that any surplus should go towards funding an exhibition dedicated to this icon.

Sealed bids meant it was impossible to find out before the deadline, and with so many bidders rumoured to be in the running earlier in the NRM's campaign to save *Flying Scotsman* for the nation, there was a chance it could stay in private hands.

The NRM put in a bid of £2.2 million and then had to sit back and wait patiently until 2 April, when bids were finally submitted. It took three long days for the winner to be announced. On 5 April, Scott, the NRM and the public received the news that they had been so desperately hoping for: the public bid for *Flying Scotsman* had finally been chosen. After decades of being the 'people's engine' in their hearts, finally, she really was the people's engine in every sense of the word.

Seven bidders put in offers for *Flying Scotsman* starting at £600,000, around the accepted value of a locomotive of similar size. The sale price included the spare 'A4' boiler, a spare cylinder from former classmate No. 60041 *Salmon Trout* and other useful parts. Her future was now secure, and the NRM even had some spare money to finance the engine's operation. In the final analysis, the fund consisted of £365,000 donated by the public and matched by Sir Richard Branson, £1.8 million from the NHMF and £600,000 from Yorkshire Forward.

Those anticipating an immediate return to traffic would be disappointed as there were some mechanical issues to resolve, but after forty-one years in private ownership the locomotive was now safe, and would be safe for the nation to marvel at for years to come.

Forty-one years earlier, Alan Pegler had saved *Flying Scotsman* from the cutter's torch when she was withdrawn from British Railways' service with just a few weeks' notice for interested parties to raise funds. He was overjoyed with the news saying: 'Everything has come out exactly as I hoped,' he said. 'I was so damned excited after I heard the news that I hardly slept, and I was up at the crack of dawn to hear the first BBC news bulletin at 6.10am.'

With *Flying Scotsman* under National Railway Museum (NRM) ownership, the museum announced plans to make her the central attraction at its major nine-day Railfest event to celebrate 200 years since the first successful steam locomotive was built way back in 1804. With the public in mind, following the huge number of donations received, the NRM followed up its pledge to make *Flying Scotsman* accessible to everyone by planning a series of budget priced, York to Scarborough trains to take day trippers from the NRM's home to the east coast town.

Her new home at the NRM and the plans for the immediate future offered a slightly more sedate pace of life for *Flying Scotsman*. Though some thought this was a waste of a powerful engine, as well as wanting to continue with *Flying Scotsman* in operational condition, the NRM also had a duty to maintain the best interests of the then eighty-one-year-old machine. Any plans to send *Flying Scotsman* to heritage railways were partly limited by the fact that

Below In a blaze of glory and accompanied by pipers *Flying Scotsman* arrives at Railfest in York on 29 May. The diesel behind is a give-away: *Flying Scotsman* was far from ready to return to steam.

Opposite Once teething troubles were resolved No. 4472 settled into a regular duty running from York to nearby Scarborough and back. The locomotive departs for the seaside town on the 'Ride the legend' 2004 season.

when the NRM bought her, the 'Pacific' was only equipped with air-braking – vacuum brake equipment having been removed during her last overhaul. This meant that the only place to make use of *Flying Scotsman* was on the main line: a difficult and expensive task, but the NRM was keen to stress that No. 4472 would continue to be used.

Even though *Flying Scotsman* had been maintained and operated professionally when she came into NRM ownership there were some teething troubles, and none more public than her debut appearance following the sale at the NRM's major nine-day rail festival – Railfest. Completion of *Flying Scotsman's* sale had come during the final run-up to the event, and the NRM wanted to mark the locomotive's homecoming at the opening ceremony.

Sadly, the plan didn't work out. The museum had planned a special VIP train to run from Doncaster to York hauled by its new acquisition, but during preparations the evening before the run at Doncaster revealed several leaking boiler tubes that prevented the 'Pacific' from running safely at the head of a train. That meant a hasty

change of plan was brought into play. *Flying Scotsman* was towed from Doncaster to York by a diesel locomotive ready for the next day.

On the official opening day of Railfest, 29 May 2004, *Flying Scotsman* was due to break through a banner under her own power, but in the event she was propelled through by former Royal Train Class '47' No. 47798 *Prince William* – also now part of the National Collection. Thousands were there to witness *Flying Scotsman's* triumphant return to national ownership, and nobody seemed to mind that on this occasion she wasn't running under her own power. It was a defining moment in the locomotive's history. It was now official that *Flying Scotsman* was part of the National Collection and that she was here to stay.

Following Railfest, *Flying Scotsman* was taken into the museum's workshops for urgent repairs to make her fit for a return to active duty at the head of the planned series of summer trains between York and Scarborough, which started on 20 July. The damage was worse than expected and immediately after spending £2.2 million buying the 1923 engine, the NRM had to pay out another £20,000 to replace every single small tube in the boiler after the discovery of a split tube during an inspection. The failed tube had been fitted during the engine's last overhaul in 1999 and had given five years' loyal service.

With tickets on the York to Scarborough trains costing £25 per adult *Flying Scotsman* was now much more accessible and on 20 July 2004 *Flying Scotsman* resumed her trips to the seaside. It was a big contrast with the high-priced Venice-Simplon Orient Express (VSOE) work but there is no doubt this was the right approach.

Reliability problems mounted though: the work on the heavy VSOE trains had taken its toll. Mid-way through the 2004 season concerns were raised over the condition of an old repair to a crack in the cylinders of *Flying Scotsman*. Consideration was given to withdrawing the locomotive a year early to sort these problems out but she soldiered on through that first season and gave the NRM a £100,000 operating profit on the trains – a good return.

A programme of winter repairs was planned by the NRM to prepare the locomotive for the 2005 season of 'Ride the Legend' trains on the same route as in 2004,

Below *Flying Scotsman* threads through the outskirts of York to Scarborough. These trains proved highly popular and were very fairly priced.

Opposite Alan Pegler rests on the footplate of *Flying Scotsman* shortly after her acquisition by the National Railway Museum (NRM). He always said he bought the locomotive for the nation because the nation was unwilling to do so itself and was vindicated in 2004.

but before that, the apple-green 'Pacific' had two very different trains pencilled in for the autumn: the first a date with Prime Minister Tony Blair and the opening of the new NRM outpost at Shildon – Locomotion – and the second a main line trial run with the engine's former second tender that was nearing completion at the Mid-Hants Railway for Jeremy Hosking.

The trip to Shildon was a great opportunity to use such a well-known and respected steam locomotive. Tony Blair was due to perform the opening ceremony at Shildon and with *Flying Scotsman* hauling the train it couldn't have been a better plan. Sadly, it didn't come together, as more repairs were necessary before the locomotive could be used on the main line again. In the event Stanier London, Midlands and Scottish Railway 'Duchess' No. 6233 *Duchess of Sutherland* took *Flying Scotsman*'s place at the head of the prestigious train. *Flying Scotsman* was made available for the opening, but had to be a static exhibit at the opening of the £11 million Locomotion complex.

In November and back in the workshops, *Flying Scotsman* was undergoing the process of being prepared for a return to steam in May 2005, ready for the next season of 'Ride the Legend' trips to Scarborough. A list of ninety repair jobs was drawn up by the museum, ranging from welding up the crack in the cylinder and overhauling the lubrication system, to replacement of firebox crown stays and remachining the piston heads. It was a daunting task, but the success of the 2004 season must have been a great aid to getting the job done.

This time there were two halves to the 'Ride the Legend' budget trips with *Flying Scotsman*. First the trains were due to run between 31 May and 2 June, then for three days from 3–5 July *Flying Scotsman* would be on display in the museum. The main season started on 5 July and ran until 8 September: that's a total of nine weeks, running three days a week.

Through a massive effort by workshop staff and volunteers at York, *Flying Scotsman* was back in one piece and ready for a trial run on 24 May. Seven days later she was standing in York station under the wonderful and original trainshed roof waiting to depart with her first revenue-earning train of the year. It started well, but again, *Flying Scotsman*'s reliability proved problematic – she really needed a major overhaul.

In September *Flying Scotsman* was on display only for the masses at Crewe Works Open Weekend, which saw almost 30,000 people visit the show and see the apple-green 'A3' close up. The locomotive's final duties before retiring for the planned major overhaul were a series of sell-out specials operated by Tyseley-based Vintage Trains. As ever, *Flying Scotsman* was a massive draw and it was fitting to see the engine hard at work right up to the point when she returned to York for the overhaul to begin. It would prove a long and massively expensive haul to get her back up and running. Repeated return to steam targets were missed and two of the people who most influenced *Flying Scotsman*'s future passed away without seeing the locomotive return to steam again.

Tony Marchington, the man who bought the locomotive from Sir William McAlpine and Pete Waterman in 1996, passed away in October 2011 aged just 55. *Flying Scotsman's* first owner, Alan Pegler, always hoped to see the locomotive he lavished so much money and emotion on return to steam one final time but he too was denied, passing away in March 2012. He had been in poor health for some years, but his passion for steam was forever undiminished, and to the end he was perhaps the locomotive's finest ambassador and greatest supporter of all. Pegler's importance to what we now know as railway preservation cannot be understated. His drive and dedication to the Ffestiniog Railway proved that it was possible to resurrect a closed railway and without that impetus the preservationists who followed in the 1960s and beyond would have found it immeasurably more difficult to reopen the likes of the Bluebell, Keighley and Worth Valley and those other embryonic heritage railways.

But it is without doubt the spectacle of main line steam that owes most to Alan Pegler. Today anyone who can afford to acquire, overhaul and certify a steam locomotive can – providing the necessary legal and technical conditions are met – operate it at up to 75mph on any route the locomotive is cleared for and for which there is space in the timetable. Had Pegler not had the brio – not to mention cheek – to negotiate his unique deal with British Railways (BR) and face down Dr Beeching it is hard to imagine the

Below The planned return to steam dates of *Flying Scotsman's* latest overhaul came and went. In June 2011 she was unveiled in wartime black with the number 103. Anticipation was high that she would run soon after but more problems were uncovered that took a great deal of work to resolve.

Opposite A close-up of *Flying Scotsman's* nameplates in wartime condition: the background was painted black too.

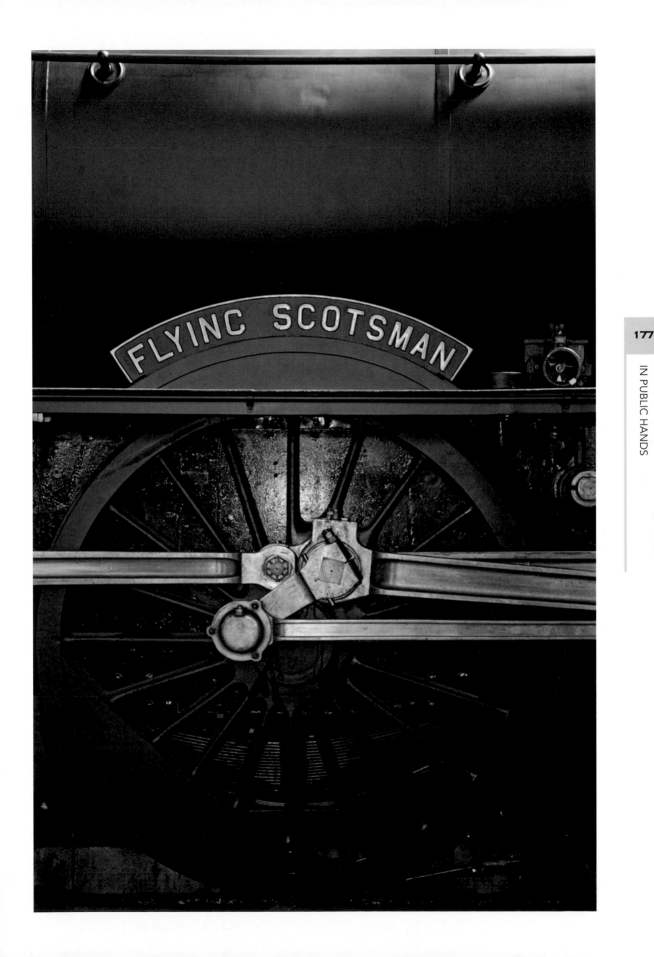

astonishing change of heart to steam that BR had in the 1970s. Without those astonishing scenes of support – the crowds who flocked to see No. 4472 in the 1960s even though it was possible until 1968 to see steam in front line service – it is almost impossible to imagine a climate that allowed Peter Prior to persuade BR that operating No. 6000 *King George V* would be a useful and powerful publicity tool. Without Pegler, it is entirely possible to suggest that steam would have been restricted to heritage railways and a maximum speed of 25mph. His place in history is assured.

It would be interesting to hear his and Marchington's take on events because until the end of 2015 the locomotive was in an awkward form of stasis undergoing an overhaul that has just gone on and on and on, every year seeming to bring fresh surprises about her condition – few of them good.

In July 2007, about the time of the first edition of this book's publication, the NRM admitted that the overhaul of the locomotive would take another eighteen months,

Below Much of *Flying Scotsman's* initial restoration was undertaken at the NRM's workshops. But as time went on more faults were discovered and the bills were rising. It would be completed elsewhere.

Opposite With the boiler removed the internal workings of *Flying Scotsman* become much clearer. The smokebox sits on the rounded saddle at the front of the locomotive.

blamed largely on the need to acquire 'a special type of copper' for the new firebox required for the locomotive's original 'A3' type boiler. Then in 2009, following trial fitment of the boiler to the locomotive frames, faulty welding was discovered in the new inner firebox delaying completion further.

But although delayed, progress seemed good. The boiler was successfully steam tested in early 2011 and at this stage the road seemed clear for a fairly rapid return to action. Indeed, in May 2011 the locomotive was repainted temporarily in Second World War black, before final commissioning and test runs. It was looking good for a spectacular and very different return to traffic.

Then a major bombshell was discovered at Ian Riley Engineering in Bury, which was restoring the locomotive. Cracks were discovered in the frame hornblocks – the components which support the driving wheel axleboxes. Having just rewheeled the locomotive and assembled the complex valve gear and motion the decision was taken to lift the locomotive from the wheels again and

check the frames ultrasonically for cracks. The testing revealed the worst: the horizontal frame stretchers which connect the two side plates were cracked and two were beyond repair. The inside cylinder motion bracket – a vital component which helps to support the valve gear – was also condemned. The delays to the overhaul were already adding to the costs but the need to make new components unexpectedly added to this further. Then the NRM acknowledged that the locomotive's main frames were 'out of true' – essentially meaning that the locomotive could have a tendency to move sideways as well as forwards and backwards – adding to the complications. The locomotive was stripped again and the fears about the frames were found to be true: they were incorrectly aligned, and before a return to traffic could be contemplated this would have to be addressed.

At the NRM and its parent organisation the National Museum of Science and Industry alarm bells were ringing loud and clear about the rising costs and widening scope of the locomotive's overhaul.

In 2012 the NRM commissioned two reports about the locomotive: one from the highly respected locomotive engineer Bob Meanley about the overhaul's problems, and another from the equally respected consultancy First Class Partnerships (FCP) about how *Flying Scotsman's* overhaul should be completed and the locomotive operated in the future. They shone an awkward and critical light on proceedings, but given the pressures and criticism the museum faced were vital in getting *Flying Scotsman* back on track.

Meanley's report came out first and true to form he didn't pull any punches. Before the NRM submitted its bid to acquire *Flying Scotsman* it commissioned a mechanical examination of the locomotive's condition. Clearly the bid submitted would be affected if the report had found *Flying Scotsman* to be in need of the massive overhaul it had now undergone. Yet AEA Technology, the body responsible for clearing *Flying Scotsman* to operate on the main line, found that its condition was largely satisfactory – a finding that has since been proved erroneous. Meanley was careful to point out that 'there is no suggestion that AEA intentionally distorted its findings to give a positive impression,' but noted that the company had been the Vehicle Acceptance Body for the locomotive for fourteen years during which it had cleared it to operate on the main line. 'Suddenly to identify a number of long-standing faults could have raised questions on its work over the previous decade,' he said.

Meanley acknowledged pressures on the NRM to operate the locomotive as much as possible following the campaign to save it, with repairs being undertaken as problems arose. Some of the work the NRM had to undertake should never have been needed though: incorrectly fitted piston rods, a welded shut mudhole and inoperable tender handbrake were all issues that the locomotive should never have had to begin with.

Although the problems with *Flying Scotsman's* boiler at the time of acquisition were quickly recognised and a lot of work undertaken, with the spare boiler earmarked for overhaul, it seems surprising that the more fundamental issues of frame cracks and misalignment were not identified. Had any of the cracked components failed on the main line the results could have been catastrophic for the locomotive, the passengers on the train it was hauling and place huge question marks about the safety and viability of operating historic machines on the main line network.

One of the most concerning aspects of the frame issues was that had the NRM stripped down the locomotive on arrival at York, many of the cracks could have been spotted earlier, and if not then certainly when the frames had been stripped to bare metal. Meanley quoted an unnamed NRM manager as saying: 'With regard to finding the defects in the hornblocks, stretchers and motion brackets – this was met by all parties with almost disbelief and extreme disappointment.'

A contract manager was appointed earlier in the restoration but following the discovery of the cracks a provisional estimate of timescale and costs was – for whatever reason – apparently accepted as the final version with no further defects expected. Problems seemed to be being discovered as the overhaul progressed: only when partially finished components were offered to the frame plates was misalignment identified.

Meanley also concluded that the NRM didn't have sufficient engineering expertise to overhaul and operate an elderly locomotive on the main line. As he pointed out, while many heritage railways rely on a handful of experienced and capable staff, the NRM *isn't* a heritage railway: it's a national organisation that has to do things rather differently. It must be remembered that in what many remember as the glory days of the 1980s, when locomotives such as *Duchess of Hamilton, Evening Star, Mallard* and others from the NRM collection took to the main line, the machines themselves were possibly in better condition – certainly they had seen less use – and that there were many staff on the railway and the NRM itself who had worked with steam traction while it was in front line service. That was a generation ago and the inevitable process of ageing and retirements meant that there were few if any full-time staff on the railway who worked meaningfully around steam. Add to that vastly changed legislative, safety and operational environments, and it was clear that for the NRM to operate and overhaul *Flying Scotsman* today required a vastly different organisation from that of the 1980s. And the question had to be asked – should it invest in the staff and facilities to do so? The NRM's role is to conserve and interpret Britain's railway history for the nation: must it also be required to overhaul, restore and operate some of its exhibits on the main line too? Had the heritage railway movement not taken off in the way that it had (and even in the 1980s few would have predicted just how vast and capable it would become) there would be a strong argument. Today, with so many heritage railways and so many steam locomotives cleared for main line operation, it is possible to argue that the NRM should focus on the exhibits in York and its Shildon outstation and leave others to undertake the operation.

This was one of the fundamental questions asked by the FCP study, which was tasked with making recommendations about the future of the overhaul, and of how the locomotive should be operated when it eventually returned to steam.

The report is, to an extent, an exercise in redaction, particularly when it comes to costs. But in terms of the engineering analysis FCP backed Meanley's findings with detail and operating insight. FCP blamed *Flying Scotsman's* mechanical condition squarely on an earlier decision to operate the locomotive with the 'A4' boiler at a higher pressure and with wider cylinder bores than it was designed for, combined with the misalignment of the middle cylinder. The report recommended that the section of frames that cannot be seen until the middle cylinder is removed should be ultrasonically tested. Riley and Sons won the tender to complete the restoration, which in autumn 2013 anticipated a relatively straightforward realignment of the inside cylinder, and at this point the NRM offered a tentative summer 2015 return to traffic for No. 4472.

It was a good job that it was cautious because in summer 2014 the investigation of the frames around the inside cylinder revealed that the misalignment was so bad that sections of new frames were needed. It wasn't merely the alignment issues that forced this decision: mounting holes had been elongated over the years, and while it would have been possible to repair these with welding it would at best have been something of a patch and repair job. But with the new sections welded to the original frames, and the way clear for installation of the cylinders, finally the locomotive was approaching a fit state.

FCP also looked at how the NRM should operate *Flying Scotsman* and if its recommendations are followed we should be looking at around 26 trips per year on a range of routes. One of the key concerns is to avoid overstretching the locomotive: she may have hauled heavier loads in the past but she is now a ninety-two-year-old machine that will be operating at up to 75mph. The need is to balance financial viability with conserving her operational lifespan. 'Maximum speed … and main line route timings should be such that the locomotive does not need to be driven at anywhere near its maximum potential,' the report said.

The total cost of the overhaul is £4.2 million – far and away the most expensive ever and possibly as much as the cost of building her close cousin No. 60163 *Tornado*, which was completed in 2008, albeit over a longer period and with much volunteer labour.

Opposite Michael O'Conner, Works Foreman for Heritage Painting, is watched by his daughter and colleague Teriann as he paints the number 60103 on the cab of *Flying Scotsman* at the NRM on 17 February 2016.

Following pages *Flying Scotsman* stands in North Yard at the National Railway Museum after its inaugural run on the East Coast Main Line on 25 February 2016. Although trespassers marred the trip and delayed No. 60103 and other service trains, the locomotive returned home to a rapturous reception.

With the overhaul under control the NRM took a decision that rankled with those who believe she should be painted in London and North Eastern Railway apple green. It opted to return her to traffic in her last front line livery of BR Brunswick Green and numbered 60103, a livery in which she appeared for a few years during the 1990s. From an historical point of view, the NRM made the only correct decision. If the museum's remit is to showcase exhibits in appropriate condition, then that which most represents *Flying Scotsman's* front line career is her last, complete with German-style smoke deflectors to lift the exhaust above the cab. It may not please everyone but it is historically the most accurate appearance of all. Other owners of locomotives can paint their machines in whatever colour they like, or give them temporary alternative identities to commemorate lost classmates if they wish, but the NRM has a duty to show things as they are rather than as people might wish they were.

After a decade-long overhaul *Flying Scotsman* finally returned to steam at the East Lancashire Railway on 7 January 2016 to begin running-in. If anyone had any doubts about her appeal to the public after such a long

Opposite This inaugural run raised eyebrows with a £450 ticket price – and trespassers put themselves at risk and delayed dozens of service trains at St Neots. The concerns about the risk of trespassers was such that Network Rail suspended publication of the locomotive's movements for a while.

Below On its first run from London King's Cross in more than a decade, *Flying Scotsman* departs for York on 25 February 2016 to a crowd of thousands.

time out of the limelight they were blown away by the reception. Media coverage approached saturation point and anticipation reached fever pitch for her first main line run between Carnforth and Carlisle on 6 February. The reception was rapturous and the locomotive proved her ability to handle main line work again. It was time to return home.

On 26 February she sallied forth from London King's Cross on her way back to York. Hype had been building up for weeks and King's Cross was as crowded as it was in 1963 on *Flying Scotsman's* last run in BR service. So was every other station on the East Coast Main Line between London and York, with railway staff positioned on platforms to ensure the public's safety.

She departed King's Cross at 07:41 in a spirit of celebration but it turned sour at St Neots when well-wishers trespassed onto this 125mph electrified railway to get as close as possible. They accessed the route at level crossings but such were the concerns that *Flying Scotsman* had to make an unscheduled stop for 10 minutes while the trespassers were encouraged off the railway. She eventually arrived in York at 13:17, 51 minutes late.

Again, trespassers wanting to see *Flying Scotsman* close up had caused real safety issues: what if one of them had been run over by a service train or the locomotive herself? There were other consequences too: fifty-nine other trains were delayed by a total of 516 minutes, leaving Network Rail with an estimated £60,000 bill to train operators.

While the NRM took the responsible decision not to publish the train's timetable, such information isn't hard to come by, and local media all along the route broadcast the timings. Unlike in the 1980s, this did not cause a question mark about the future of main line steam operation: open access rules would make an outright ban difficult and the Office of Rail and Road viewed the trespass as a one-off incident.

However, should the worst happen and a member of the public is injured or killed trying to see *Flying Scotsman,* restrictions may have to be placed on her operation. A tour from London to Victoria planned for 25 May 2016 was cancelled precisely because of those concerns. Repeats of trespass could lead to further cancellations.

Nonetheless, *Flying Scotsman* has a manageably full itinerary of main line tours ahead at the time of writing, and her first visit to a heritage railway since overhaul – the North Yorkshire Moors Railway from 12–20 March proved remarkably successful. The public desire to see and travel behind the locomotive is so great that the Severn Valley Railway rearranged its annual Autumn Steam Gala to focus

Left *Flying Scotsman* stands at North Yard at the NRM in York on 25 February 2016. The young men on the right surely didn't fire the locomotive from King's Cross – their overalls look much too clean!

60103

LONDON & NORTH EASTERN
Nº 1564
DONCASTER
1923
RAILWAY Cº

Above The first heritage railway *Flying Scotsman* visited was the North Yorkshire Moors Railway from 12–20 March 2016. On 11 March she stands at the beautifully restored station at Pickering shortly after arrival.

on *Flying Scotsman*, and such was demand that tickets to travel behind her had sold out by April – five months before the event. In fact, at the time of writing, just one opportunity to travel behind *Flying Scotsman* on the main line was available – a four-day tour which on its final day sees the London and North Eastern Railway (LNER) 'Pacific' run from Chester to London Paddington.

There are real challenges for the NRM in running *Flying Scotsman*. How can it make the locomotive accessible to travel behind without alienating visitors to York? How can it recoup those enormous overhaul costs? The decision to make the inaugural East Coast Main Line trip on 26 February a £450-per-head affair caused some raised eyebrows: shouldn't those who supported the Save Our Scotsman appeal have been given first refusal and at a more sensible price? There is, after all, plenty of time to run premium trains and there will be no shortage of interest in those.

What happens at the next overhaul? How will that be funded? Can the general public really be expected to dip into their pockets again? If not, should taxpayers who fund the NRM be expected to foot the bill?

There are no easy answers to any of these questions. It has not been an easy decade for the locomotive or the NRM and I know that one of the big concerns of staff there for a long time has been that people who contributed to the Save Our Scotsman fund may not now be alive to see her running again. But I think that on balance, whether supporters and donors are with us or not, they would rather the NRM took the time to restore the locomotive properly and to the highest standards possible, addressing technical issues that may well have devilled the locomotive for many decades, and giving her the best possible chance of stretching her legs on the main line where she belongs.

Her place in railway history from a technical and operational standpoint remains every bit as valid as when the NRM acquired her, and with more than half a century having passed since her preservation, she stands as a vital and fundamental marker in that story too.

Like many, many others I was thrilled by *Flying Scotsman's* return to steam and I am looking forward to watching her lope by at speed from the lineside and travelling behind her on a main line run. It has been a very long wait, but I have no doubt that it's been worth it. Gresley, Sparshatt, Pegler, Marchington and all those others no longer with us who played such important roles in her history would agree too, of that I am sure.

I thought when I started writing this book that I would be able to find some simple answers to why *Flying Scotsman* is so famous. From her construction, to Wembley and then Sparshatt's marvellous sprint down Stoke Bank; the last-minute escape from the cutter's torch, the contrast with the embers of BR steam; the American adventure – and her consequent rescue and second life under Bill McAlpine, all of these facets have burnished the aura and cemented the legend.

But I don't think these completely why *Flying Scotsman* is so well-known and loved. I think a lot of it goes back to the LNER's inspired decision to give the locomotive such a heart-achingly evocative name, and then to produce some of the most brilliant and stylish marketing of her namesake train throughout the 1920s and 1930s. So good was this marketing that I think it created a cultural memory so strong that fifteen years after the LNER ceased to exist, many thousands went to pay their last respects on her last run in public ownership.

The media has also played a part right from the very start. For a long time, *Flying Scotsman* and her sister locomotives were just about the biggest passenger locomotives in Britain: a kind of national flagship of the railways, and they attracted great interest. And once steam was on the way out, *Flying Scotsman* became a good, slightly quirky story for the media to cover: after all, it's not every day that a famous steam locomotive departs to and returns from America and Australia!

She is, to very many people, the epitome of what a steam locomotive should look like and of the gloss, glitz and glamour of that long-gone golden age of the railway between the wars. *Flying Scotsman* has achieved such incredible feats, been through so much, and despite repeated threats to her future, somehow, she has always survived. In the process she has become a kind of talisman for railway preservation, for steam and of the railway itself. If I had to choose a single locomotive to represent the age of steam and its engineering, operation, marketing and social effects two hundred years hence, it would be *Flying Scotsman* without question.

Generally speaking, Britain is a nation of shopkeepers but we're inordinately proud about of our engineering marvels: *Flying Scotsman*, the Spitfire, E-Type Jag, Concorde … they all transcend the boundary between engineering and art in a way that little else can. Which other country could possibly have produced such icons?

Flying Scotsman sums up the very best of British ingenuity, dedication, passion, bloody-mindedness and brilliance – and now she can roam the rails with a secure future and an adoring public. It's been an extraordinary story and now that she's running again it's a story that will continue to enthral millions of people all over the world. Britain and its railways should be extremely proud of this remarkable machine.

Following pages The moment so many millions had been waiting for: *Flying Scotsman* makes her first main line test run on 6 February 2016, pictured near the stunning Ribblehead Viaduct on the Settle to Carlisle line – one of her regular haunts during the 1970s and 1980s.

CREDITS

Every effort has been made to credit the copyright holders of the images used in this book. We apologise for any unintentional omissions or errors and would be pleased to insert the appropriate acknowledgement to any companies or individuals in any subsequent editions of the work.

PHOTO LIBRARY CREDITS

4: Leo Marfurt/Advertising Archive, **5:** National Railway Museum /Science & Society Picture Library, **6–7:** Science & Society Picture Library/Getty Images, **12-13:** Daily Herald Archive/National Media Museum / Science & Society Picture Library, **14:** AP/Topfoto, **16-17:** National Railway Museum/Science & Society Picture Library, **18:** National Railway Museum/Science & Society Picture Library, **19:** Science & Society Picture Library, **20-21:** National Railway Museum / Science & Society Picture Library, **22:** National Railway Museum/ Science & Society Picture Library, **23:** Museum of Science and Industry, Chicago/Getty Images, **24-25:** NRM/ Pictorial Collection/Science & Society Picture Library, **27t:** Artmedia/Heritage Images/TopFoto, **27b:** Brooke/Stringer/ Getty Images, **29:** The Montifraulo Collection, **30-31:** Onslow Auctions Collection/Mary Evans Picture Library, **33:** Topical Press Agency/Getty Images, **36:** National Railway Museum/ Science & Society Picture Library, **37l:** H L Oakley/Mary Evans Picture Library, **37r:** National Railway Museum/ Science & Society Picture Library, **38-40:** NRM/Pictorial Collection/ Science & Society Picture Library, **42t:** Science & Society Picture Library/ Getty Images, **43:** National Railway Museum/Science & Society Picture Library, **45:** Moviestore Collection/REX/ Shutterstock, **46:** Interfoto/Sammlung Rauch/Mary Evans Picture Library, **47:** Ullstein Bild / Topfoto, **48-49:** Science & Society Picture Library/Getty Images, **50:** Douglas Miller / Getty Images, **53:** NRM/Pictorial Collection/ Science & Society Picture Library, **54:** Imagno/Mary Evans Picture Library, **56:** National Railway Museum/Science & Society Picture Library, **57:** Science & Society Picture Library/Getty Images, **58:** Daily Herald Archive/NMEM/ Science & Society Picture Library, **60-61:** National Railway Museum/ Science & Society Picture Library, **62:** Barry Bateman/Alamy, **63:** Science & Society Picture Library/Getty Images,

69: Science & Society Picture Library/ Getty Images, **71:** Science & Society Picture Library/Getty Images, **73:** DK/ National Railway Museum/Science & Society Picture Library, **77:** Three Lions/ Getty Images, **78:** National Railway Museum/Science & Society Picture Library, **80:** VisitBritain/Britain on View/Getty Images, **86:** Science & Society Picture Library/Getty Images, **87:** Science & Society Picture Library, **88-89:** Paul Walters Worldwide Photography/HIP/TopFoto, **95:** Daily Herald Archive/National Media Museum/Science & Society Picture Library, **97:** Terence Cuneo/Bridgeman Images, **102:** Science & Society Picture Library/Getty Images, **103:** Science & Society Picture Library/Getty Images, **105:** Ron Case /Getty Images, **106:** Daily Mail/REX/ Shutterstock, **107:** Topfoto, **112:** Mike Condren, **115:** Trinity Mirror/Mirrorpix/ Alamy, **116:** Keystone Pictures USA / Alamy, **118:** Emery Gulash / Morning Sun/Science & Society Picture Library, **119:** National Railway Museum/Getty Images, **121:** Emery Gulash/Morning Sun/Science & Society Picture Library, **122:** Mike Condren, **125:** Mike Condren, **129:** Manchester Daily Express/Science & Society Picture Library, **130:** David McHugh/REX/Shutterstock, **131:** P Bucknall/Alamy, **134:** NRM/Pictorial Collection/Science & Society Picture Library, **136:** Daily Herald Archive/ National Media Museum/Science & Society Picture Library, **139:** National Railway Museum/Science & Society Picture Library, **143:** Local World/REX/ Shutterstock, **144:** Paul Mayall/REX/ Shutterstock, **145:** National Railway Museum / Science & Society Picture Library, **146:** Rail Heritage WA/Science & Society Picture Library, **147:** Rail Heritage WA/Science & Society Picture Library, **148:** Rail Heritage WA/Science & Society Picture Library, **149:** Sydney Morning Herald/ Science & Society Picture Library, **150-151:** Paul Nevin/Getty Images **152:** Photofusion/Getty Images, **153-154:** REX/Shutterstock, **156:** Peter Price REX/Shutterstock, **158:** Richard Wintle/ REX/Shutterstock, **160:** UPP/Topfoto, **161-163:** REX/Shutterstock, **165t:** Andy Rain/epa/Corbis, **163b:** Katie Garrod/ JAI/Corbis, **166:** Wiki Commons, **168:** Odd Andersen/Getty Images, **169:** National Railway Museum/Science & Society Picture Library, **170:** Odd Andersen/Getty Images, **172:** National

Railway Museum/Science & Society Picture Library, **173:** National Railway Museum/Getty Images, **174:** Science & Society Picture Library/Getty Images, **175:** Pete Lomas / Associated Newspapers /REX/Shutterstock, **176:** Kippa Matthews/REX/Shutterstock, **177:** National Railway Museum/ Science & Society Picture Library, **178:** Rii Schroer/REX/Shutterstock, **179:** Richard Gardner/REX/Shutterstock, **180:** Oli Scarff/Getty Images, **182:** National Railway Museum/Science & Society Picture Library, **184:** Paul Marriott/REX/Shutterstock, **185:** Toby Smith/Getty Images, **186:** National Railway Museum/Science & Society Picture Library, **188:** Dobson Agency. co.uk/REX/Shutterstock, **190-191:** Peter Furlong/Getty Images.

Thanks also to the following:

2: F.R. Hebron/Rail Archive Stephenson, **9, 82-83:** T.G. Hepburn/ Rail Archive Stephenson, **26:** W.H. Whitworth/Rail Archive Stephenson, **32, 35:** Rail Archive Stephenson, **42b:** W.J. Reynolds/Rail Archive Stephenson, **44:** C.R.L. Coles/Rail Archive Stephenson, **68:** D.M.C. Hepburne-Scott/Rail Archive Stephenson, **72:** Cecil Ord/Rail Archive Stephenson, **10-11, 138, 142:** Gavin Morrison, **28:** RAS Collection, **64-65:** P.J. Hughes/Colour-rail, **66-67, 74, 84-85t:** Colour-Rail, **84-85b,** **94:** Colin Stacey/Initial Photographics, **90-91:** J.F. Aylard/Initial Photograhics, **92, 98-99, 110-111, 132-133, 140:** Brian Stephenson, **108, 126, 128:** Peter Fitton

STAFF CREDITS

Publisher: Richard Green
Commissioning Editor: Jennifer Barr
Project Manager: Victoria Marshallsay
Picture Research: Ben White
Design: Sooky Choi
Production Controller: Robin Boothroyd